D0931550

PETER'S PORTRAIT
OF JESUS

PETER'S PORTRAIT OF JESUS

A Commentary on

THE GOSPEL OF MARK

and

THE LETTERS OF PETER

by

J. B. Phillips

Colour photographs by
Alistair Duncan

COLLINS + WORLD
Cleveland and New York
1976

William Collins + World Publishing Co., Inc.

In the text of this book "AV" refers to the
Authorised (or King James) Version

Library of Congress Catalogue Card Number
76–19154
First Published 1976
© J. B. Phillips 1976
ISBN 0 00 215628 8

Set in Intertype Baskerville
Made and Printed in Great Britain by
A. Wheaton & Co., Exeter

CONTENTS

*

ERRATUM

On page 33, 9 lines up from the foot of
the page, the line should read 'man and
he all but crawled to Jesus in the ex-
tremity of his'.

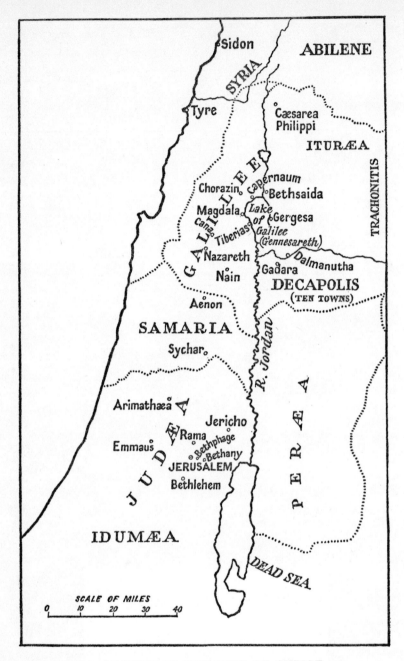

PALESTINE IN THE TIME OF CHRIST

ILLUSTRATIONS

*

INTRODUCTION

*

'Familiarity breeds contempt' says the old proverb. But it is not necessarily contempt that is produced when we become too accustomed to places, things and people. It is much more likely that our familiarity will breed a sort of indifference, even a blindness towards the worth of what we know so well and see so often. It is this kind of inability to see with any clarity, or appreciate with any conviction, which specially applies to our approach to such a work as the short Greek book known as the Gospel according to Mark. Simply because it is so readily available, in a great many languages indeed, and because most of us have known it all our lives, it is apt to be dismissed as 'part of the New Testament', and never properly valued, or indeed read with adult minds.

Yet Mark's Gospel is in fact the earliest piece of Christian propaganda that we possess, and its authenticity is hardly doubted by anyone. It is not, of course, the earliest piece of Christian writing – some of Paul's letters were written ten or more years before this little book. But it is the first piece of propaganda. The usages of war, the language of advertising and the pressures of politics have conspired to spoil the proper meaning of this word for us. By itself it carries no overtones whether good or bad. From its Latin derivation it can only mean things which ought to be spread, in the same way that seeds are spread in the sowing, and this is the early Church's first attempt to put the life and teaching of Jesus Christ together in a form that could be propagated.

The sources of Mark's writing are almost certainly the recollections of Peter. This theory is first supported by Papias, a bishop in Phrygia, who wrote in about 132, 'Mark, having

9

become the interpreter of Peter, wrote down accurately everything he remembered, without however recording in order
what was either said or done by Christ.'

Iranaeus, Bishop of Lyons, writing later in the same
century, speaks of, 'Mark the disciple and interpreter of
Peter'.

Tertullian of Carthage, writing at the beginning of the next
century about the authority of the Gospels, refers again to
Mark as Peter's interpreter.

Eusebius, the Church historian of Caesarea, writing about
the end of the third century and the beginning of the fourth,
wrote that 'Peter, by reason of excess modesty, did not under-
take to write a Gospel. It had yet all along been currently
reported that Mark, who had become his familiar acquaint-
ance and attendant, made memoirs of his discourses concern-
ing the doings of Jesus.' Then, a little later on, he writes, 'For
all the contents of Mark's Gospel are regarded as memoirs of
Peter's discourses.'

And then we come to the more familiar name of Jerome
writing at the beginning of the fifth century, who says, 'Mark,
the disciple and interpreter of Peter, wrote a brief Gospel, at
the request of the brethren in Rome, in accordance with what
he had heard related by Peter. This Gospel, when it was read
over to Peter, was approved of and published by his authority,
to be read in the churches.'

There is no particular reason to doubt these early witnesses,
and it was not long before the authenticity of the Marcan
Gospel, backed by the apostolic authority of Peter, was firmly
established throughout the Church.

Thus Mark gathered much of his material from stories that
Peter told. Of course he would have to arrange these, at least
roughly, to form a book; but his authority is Peter the
fisherman-apostle. He is using material which can be said
with confidence to be an eye-witness's account.

When *The Young Church in Action* was first published it
contained besides the translation of the Acts, an appendix

with some expanded sermons. One of these was Peter's sermon
on the day of Pentecost. It was more than a translation of
the summary given in Acts 2; it was filled out. At the points
where Peter probably illustrated his sermon or developed his
argument, material was supplied from Mark's Gospel. If you
read that expanded sermon you will see how well the material
fits together. It is a good sermon, obviously preached by one
man. This exercise alone is additional evidence for the theory
that Mark depended on Peter when he came to write his
Gospel. Then there are many passages throughout Mark's
Gospel where the word 'they' is ambiguous. Sometimes, when
it is replaced by 'we', the whole story becomes much clearer.
Now if Mark were writing down stories that Peter told, then
he would have 'we' in many places where his Gospel account
of the story would have to change the 'we' into 'they'. So
Mark is probably the Gospel that Peter would have written.
It is the earliest Gospel that we possess and it is dated
around 65.

The style of this Gospel is terse and verbally economical;
it conveys its message forcefully but with the minimum number of words. This may well be Mark's own characteristic,
but we cannot help feeling the presence of Peter, the man who
was there at the time. Peter himself may well have been
martyred in the Neronian persecutions, and it is thought by
some that this short Gospel was written under the threat of
arrest and probable death.

For years many Christians had thought of the return of
Christ as being very soon. They had interpreted certain words
of Jesus to mean that he would be back in triumph during
their lifetime. As the years went by and the leaders of the
Church died or were martyred, the hope of an immediate
return faded. Then it became obvious that, if the record of
the life of Jesus were to be preserved, it would have to be
written down very soon. Those who knew him in the flesh
were dying off rapidly. A crisis came in the winter of 64–65
when a great fire devastated Rome. Nero blamed the

Christians and ordered a persecution. (It is possible that both Peter and Paul died during this series of persecutions.) Many other Christians died also and this fact brought to a head the need to write down and preserve the stories of the life of Jesus and to make a record of his sayings.

About this time two books were written : one was a collection of sayings which has been lost but which was quoted extensively by Matthew and Luke in their Gospels. This is known as Q = *quelle* the German for 'source'. The other is Mark's Gospel. That also was quoted extensively by Matthew and Luke. This book was preserved even though most of its material was later incorporated in longer Gospels. One may wonder why it was preserved and copied. It was probably the Gospel most readily available in Rome and it was hallowed as a Gospel associated with Peter. Its title was probably the very first line of the text : that is, 'The Gospel of Jesus Christ, the Son of God'. The name of Mark was added much later. The writer tries to keep out of the picture, although he has added his signature in a little tale which otherwise has no meaning. That is the story of the young man who escaped from the soldiers' hands on the night of Jesus' arrest (Mark 14:51).

The Christian use of the word 'gospel' probably begins here. It is a new form of writing and the choice of the word is interesting. 'Gospel' means, quite simply, 'good news' and once it meant little else. But it sometimes meant some concession or gift to the people announced on the appointment of a new ruler, a royal birthday or a coronation. Mark's use of this word in his title, taken up by Matthew, Luke and John, has given to the world a new form of writing which says at once what the book contains. A Gospel, thereafter, means only one thing – an account of the good news of Christ, telling of his doings, his sayings and his significance for the world. John, who is the latest writer of the Gospels, explains very clearly what a Gospel is when he summarizes his own reasons for writing one : 'Jesus gave a great many other signs in the presence of his disciples which are not recorded in this book. But these have been written so that you may believe that Jesus is Christ, the Son of God, and that in that faith you may have life through his name' (John 20:30, 31).

JOHN MARK

The writer of this earliest Gospel was born in Jerusalem. We hear quite a lot about him and his home during the early days of the Christian Church. If the last supper took place in an upper room in John Mark's mother's house, then Mark *might* have overheard some of the conversation and Jesus' words about his own imminent death. If so, he might have left his bed and hidden, clothed only in a linen shirt, in the Garden of Gethsemane – only a guess, but fascinating!

His mother, Mary, kept open house for the early Christians and it was there that Peter went quite naturally when he was released from prison (Acts 12:12). John Mark had an unfortunate beginning to his efforts at missionary work. He was obviously deeply moved by Paul and Barnabas, his uncle, and wanted to accompany them on their missionary journeys. He was not very successful, and Paul was somewhat unsympathetic to his weakness. Even Luke, who tries to show most people in the best possible light, does not hide the fact of John Mark's desertion, 'There John left them and turned back to Jerusalem' (Acts 13:13). He continued as a Christian in Jerusalem and, when another missionary journey was proposed, he wanted again to go with Paul and Barnabas. This was an occasion for sharp dispute between the two great missionaries. Barnabas believed that when a young man had failed once he should be given a second chance. Paul thought that this was not the stuff from which missionaries were made. The dispute became so sharp that Paul and Barnabas separated (Acts 15:39). Barnabas took John Mark with him and Paul went off with Silas. They divided the mission field between them and Mark became a missionary. We hear no more about him in the Acts because Luke follows the story of Paul and Silas rather than that of Barnabas and Mark (Acts 15:36–41). The final reference to Mark seems to be in 1 Peter 5:13, 'Your sister-church here in "Babylon" sends you greetings, and so does my son Mark.' There we leave Mark, in Rome. He has been associated with the Christian community almost from the beginning, particularly if he is the young man who ran away at the arrest of Jesus (Mark 14:51).

His close association with so many of the leading Christians in those early days gave him an opportunity to ask questions and to check his stories. He seems to have been very close to Peter at the end in Rome. All this made him suitable as a reliable reporter of the life and sayings of Jesus. His main material may be from Peter, but he could scarcely fail to gather much from his long years of talking to others about Jesus, whom he had seen but did not know.

Mark's Gospel is rough and is not a polished literary work. It has the forceful vitality of a man who believes what he writes. It has flashes of realism. It draws with strong lines the portrait of a man who was both thoroughly human and unmistakably the Son of God.

We have probably lost the end of his Gospel, but there is a certain appropriateness in ending it where most of the manuscripts do, without any account of a resurrection appearance. This story ends : 'And they got out of the tomb and ran away from it. They were trembling with excitement. They did not dare to breathe a word to anyone' (Mark 16:8). Part of the roughness, of course, may come from Peter whose stories have scarcely been polished.

LETTERS OF PETER

The fisherman-apostle is so well-known that one does not need to write his story in this introduction. It is told not only in Mark, but in all the Gospels. It is continued by Luke in the Acts of the Apostles. Peter developed as a Christian leader, but seems not to have changed very much in basic temperament. His blazing outburst in Acts 8:20, for example, cannot be translated by polite phrasing! Paul was obviously angry with him more than once because he would be carried away with enthusiasm but would not always remain faithful to his promises. The anger of Paul related in Galatians 2:11 is very early, that is in 56–57, and was probably justified. Peter, who was designed by Christ to be the leader of the Church, did not in fact turn out to be much of a leader at all. He is very soon replaced by James in Jerusalem and his missionary endeavours throughout the world are taken over by Paul. He is a man full of failures and attractive, probably, because of that. He emerges from the stories in the Gospels as someone we would like to have known. He is a real man.

1 Peter is a genuine letter. It was probably a circular letter, but has the style of a man writing to people he knows and who trust him. He is writing it from a place which he calls 'Babylon'. To the Jews this was a familiar name for Rome and most people agree that Peter was writing from there. There are other theories and an attractive one is that it came from a little place called Babylon near Cairo. But there is no real weight of evidence behind that. Wherever he wrote from there were soldiers around, and this has influenced the style of his letter. Peter draws on the vocabulary of the barracks and, as he writes to Christians probably scattered by persecution or force of circumstances throughout Asia Minor, he appeals to them as a Christian army.

There is obviously a reason for writing this letter and the change of style towards the end suggests that something happened while he was writing it. The earlier part of the letter is more carefully considered as it deals with the Christian's attitude to undeserved suffering and persecution. It has almost the style of a sermon. It tells the leaders how to behave if persecution should come. It is with chapter 4:12 that the persecution seems to have come and there is more urgency about the style of the last part of the letter.

2 Peter is totally different from the other two books that we have looked at. Its style is the reverse of brief and economical in words, being often florid and rhetorical, and its teaching is somewhat remote from life. Nobody knows who wrote it except that it is quite certain that Peter did not write much of it at all! There could be fragments from Peter here, but most of the letter shows the style of the second century; possibly it is the latest thing in the New Testament. It contains a few outstanding phrases, but is one of the least profitable of the books. How it came to be associated with the name of Peter nobody knows, unless it contains fragments by the apostle.

DATES

Mark and 1 Peter are not very far removed from each other in date. 1 Peter came first and then, probably within a year or two, Mark wrote his Gospel.

2 Peter was written probably about AD 130.

All the people . . . went out to him in the desert
and received his baptism in the river Jordan,
publicly confessing their sins. (Mark 1:5)

THE GOSPEL OF
MARK

Then the Spirit sent him out at once into the
desert, and there he remained for forty days while
Satan tempted him. (Mark 1:12)

CHAPTER ONE

*

How it began

vs 1–8 The Gospel of Jesus Christ, the Son of God,
begins with the fulfilment of this prophecy of Isaiah –
> Behold, I send my messenger before thy face,
> Who shall prepare thy way;
> The voice of one crying in the wilderness,
> Make ye ready the way of the Lord,
> Make his paths straight.

For John came and began to baptize men in the
desert, proclaiming baptism as the mark of a complete
change of heart and of the forgiveness of sins. All the
people of the Judean countryside and everyone in
Jerusalem went out to him in the desert and received
his baptism in the river Jordan, publicly confessing their
sins.

John himself was dressed in camel-hair, with a leather
belt round his waist, and he lived on locusts and wild
honey. The burden of his preaching was, 'There is someone coming after me who is stronger than I – indeed
I am not good enough to kneel down and undo his shoes.
I have baptized you with water, but he will baptize you
with the Holy Spirit.'

The word Gospel comes from the Old English word Godspell,
meaning good news. There was a word evangel in English
approximating to the Greek *euaggelion*, but I have only been
able to find it in early Victorian hymns and in religious writ-
ings, and it has not lasted in the popular vocabulary.
Euaggelion meant originally the reward paid to a messenger

bringing good news, then it came to mean the good news itself. There might be, for example, the good news of the accession of a new king or governor, and sometimes this included some down-to-earth good news such as a slight reduction in taxes! But over the years it came to mean any piece of good news. Its special use by the New Testament writers is, naturally, that this is the Gospel or Good News of Jesus Christ or of God. The content of the Christian gospel is good indeed. It declares unequivocally that God loves his world, that he visited it in person in Jesus Christ; that he healed once and for all the agonizing breach between sinful man and the perfection of God; and that he overcame man's last enemy, death, thus opening the way to life beyond time and space to all who put their trust, not in themselves, but in Christ.

It should be noted that by no means all religions are good news. There is not much gospel about Hinduism, and the religion of Islam is distinctly short on good news for women. At a time when unthinking men declare that 'all religions are much the same', it is worth taking a close look at some other religions and noting their conspicuous lack of good news.

Mark here calls the man Jesus, Christ. Christ comes from a Greek word meaning the Anointed One and is almost exactly equivalent to the Hebrew word translated Messiah. In the Old Testament we note that kings, that is the chosen of God, were anointed with oil. The same custom exists today in this country and our sovereign lady Queen Elizabeth was anointed with oil in her coronation ceremony. However, the *Christos* or Christ of God was the especially chosen and appointed one and his title very quickly became indissolubly linked with his human name of Jesus.

The Son of God as a title alternates in Mark with the human title Son of Man. It is a little difficult to convey the meaning of 'Son of' common to both Greek and Hebrew, in modern English. But we should not be far wrong if we inferred that Mark means Jesus to be regarded as both God and man living as one person in the human scene.

The prophecy which Mark quotes is really a composite one, being derived from both Malachi and Isaiah. Mark gives the credit only to Isaiah, possibly as a matter of simplification, possibly because Isaiah was by far the greater and better known.

Baptism, as a form of ceremonial washing away of past sins, was a common feature of many religions. It is a simple universal outward sign, and was not despised in the unfolding purpose of God. This particular baptism was 'a baptism of repentance' which is the way the AV translates it. Two important points arise here. One is that the Greek word *metanoia* is not adequately translated by the English word repentance. It really does mean a complete change of outlook, that is a conversion of both heart and mind, and repentance assumes that men can 'repent' of their own free will and indeed in some instances in both Old and New Testaments are commanded to 'repent'. How far is this realistic? The process of change of heart and mind is plainly a possibility, for John was no fool, and his preaching obviously had result. But we are so conditioned today that we assume that an act of fundamental change in a man's character is unlikely to the point of impossibility. Are we perhaps badly misled and is the possibility which is tacitly denied every day of the week, really something which could take place in the right circumstances, at the command of the right moral authority? It is a point worth our serious thought, and we should not forget that the physical act of baptism is meaningless and even deceptive unless the *metanoia* accompanies it.

It is hard for us to imagine this mass urge for baptism and confession of sin. We need to remember all the time that the coming of the long-expected Messiah was never long absent from the minds of the Jews. It is quite natural that such a coming must be heralded by a wholesale admission of past sins and failures. We know, with the benefit of hindsight, that they were expecting the wrong kind of Messiah. They wanted someone indeed who would lead them back to the pure worship of God, but they also expected this someone to be a blazing patriot who would deliver them from the hated Roman yoke. If people are honestly expecting benefits of this kind they are going to make very sure that they do all they can to make the dream come true. The first step was repentance and baptism, and this duty they hurried to fulfil.

John was dressed simply, with both economy and utility in mind. The camel-hair robe was, and I believe is, in common use by desert-dwellers since it affords protection from the scorching heat of the sun and warmth when crouched for comfort in some cave or cleft in the rocks in nights of bitter cold. The leather girdle was a simple device to keep the robe in place when moving rapidly or when doing manual work. It was of untanned skin, as used by the Bedouins today.

John's food was similarly simple and such as the desert could provide. Locusts may seem to us a strange food, but they are in fact quite nutritious and are still eaten by the Bedouin Arabs and the poorer classes in general. We are not to make the mistake of thinking these are the luscious locust beans which would hardly have flourished in the arid desert. The species of locust allowed to be eaten by Jewish Law is mentioned in Leviticus 11:22.

We can rightly assume that John was a somewhat fierce ascetic character, but he was not in the least self-assertive. His holy task, meditated over for many months in the desert, was to make way for one infinitely greater than himself. John regarded this coming one with the most profound respect, and knew that what he was doing was almost nothing compared with what Christ would do. 'Baptism with the Holy Spirit' must have sounded novel and strange to his hearers, and without doubt sent them away thinking busily. It should have the same effect upon us.

The arrival of Jesus

vs 9–13 It was in those days that Jesus arrived from the Galilean village of Nazareth and was baptized by John in the Jordan. All at once, as he came up out of the water, he saw the heavens split open, and the Spirit coming down upon him like a dove. A voice came out of Heaven, saying,

'You are my dearly-beloved Son, in whom I am well pleased!'

Then the Spirit sent him out at once into the desert, and there he remained for forty days while Satan tempted him. During this time no one was with him but wild animals, and only the angels were there to care for him.

Mark intends this to mean that in the middle of this campaign of mass baptism Jesus arrived from Nazareth. Just as his birth occurred in the midst of human activity, so his baptism is not marked out as a special occasion; it happened as it might have done to any other devout Jew. Mark does not mention John's reluctance to baptize Jesus, his spiritual superior. He is only concerned to record the event. 'All at once' or 'suddenly' or 'immediately' are favourite words of Mark and give his narrative considerable pace. Nevertheless in this instance you could hardly have a vision of the heavens ripped open gradually or by degrees! The word used is a violent one and could be used of ripping a piece of cloth and this is in contrast with the quiet appearance of the traditional bird of peace, a dove. It is perhaps worth noting here that images both of gentleness and violent energy can be found in many places in the New Testament. We should be wrong to conclude that the work of the Spirit is always gentle as in the suggestion of the hymn which says: 'his that gentle voice we hear, soft as the breath of even, which checks each fault and calms each fear and speaks of Heaven.'

The voice from Heaven was probably only understood by Jesus himself. This direct message from God must have been of enormous comfort to him. Such a direct message occurs only three times as far as the records show: at his baptism, at his Transfiguration and on the occasion of the Greeks seeking him, a critical point in his ministry, assuring Jesus that his call was not merely for the Jews. See John 12:29. For we are not to suppose, I think, that he went through life without doubts and questionings. The people around may have indeed heard a loud noise and remarked 'it thundered' as John's Gospel records in somewhat similar circumstances.

Now the Spirit positively *drives* Jesus into the desert. The Greek word *ekballo* is translated in the AV by nearly a dozen different English words, but they all contain the notion of remorseless and sometimes violent movement. The forty days which Jesus spent alone in the desert were a period of intense temptation, and doubtless, in spite of the direct voice from Heaven which he had just heard, a period of agonized prayer. Some hints of the general lines of the temptation were passed on later by Jesus to his disciples, but these are not mentioned by Mark. It does not require much imagination to see how, during a period of long fasting, Jesus could be subjected to terrifying and concentrated attacks from the Prince of Evil himself. There must have been deep misgivings as to the certainty of his vocation, fear-filled doubts as the apparent impossibility of his mission began to take more definite shape, and anxiety about his own ability to withstand the intolerable burden that was inescapably his. Mark goes into no details but with telling economy he mentions the wild animals and the angels. We are not, I am convinced, to think of the wild animals in some sentimental St Francis of Assisi-like dumb friends league. There were, and are, cheetahs, boars, jackals, wolves, hyenas, etc., which could only add to his sense of danger and loneliness. What the angels did is not clear, but angels, which by definition are simply messengers, are not to be thought of in terms of stained-glass windows and children's picture books. Throughout the Bible in both testaments God occasionally allows these messengers to pass from Heaven to earth. To say more than that would be simply guesswork, but the use of the imperfect tense implies that there was more than one visit over the period of the temptation, and that the heavenly messengers helped Jesus.

Jesus begins to preach the gospel . . .

vs 14, 15 It was after John's arrest that Jesus came into Galilee, proclaiming the gospel of God, saying,

'The time has come at last – the kingdom of God has arrived. You must change your hearts and minds and believe the good news.'

We are now six weeks later. The story of John's imprisonment is told by Mark a little later in 6:17 and perhaps it is only mentioned here to emphasize that Jesus began his ministry alone. He proclaims what is now called the Gospel of God. There is, of course, no difference at all in meaning between the two expressions, the Gospel of God and the Gospel of Jesus Christ.

The Good News is God's declaration and the content of the Good News is of Jesus Christ himself. Here again we have the command to change hearts and minds, not so much now in preparation but because the kingdom of God has actually arrived. The readers of Mark's Gospel would know perfectly well the content of the 'good news'.

Perhaps we should note that from the very beginning the acceptance of God's kingdom means an act of faith.

. . . and to call men to follow him

vs 16–20 As he walked along the shore of the Lake of Galilee, he saw two fishermen, Simon and his brother Andrew, casting their nets into the water.

'Come and follow me, and I will teach you to catch men!' he cried.

At once they dropped their nets, and followed him.

Then he went a little further along the shore and saw James the son of Zebedee, aboard a boat with his brother John, overhauling their nets. At once he called them, and they left their father Zebedee in the boat with the hired men, and went off after him.

Jesus finds Simon and his brother Andrew throwing their hand-nets in the shallow water by the shore of the lake. They may have been washing their nets, or simply casting around in a desultory fashion hoping for the chance of some fish venturing inshore. (It goes without saying that these small nets were quite different from the large drag-net which was used in an operation similar to our modern trawling.)

The sudden, almost peremptory, command of Jesus has a strong dramatic effect. Into a scene of men's leisure comes the call to leave their usual work completely, follow a man hitherto unknown to them as far as we know, and change their whole way of living. The edge of humour in Jesus' crisp command is a natural touch, and reveals a side to his character which occurs several times in the Gospel accounts.

Mark does not comment in any way on this strange sudden action on the part of Jesus. But we who read the words many years later find our minds filled with questions. Was this man, who could so invite men to follow him, someone of outstanding personal magnetism? Was this a voice filled with such authority that men of goodwill could not help but respond to him? Can we imagine the sheer force of a totally integrated personality completely dedicated to his Father's will? Certainly we must at once recognize the tremendous authority of Jesus. People recognized it in his speaking as we shall see and it is equally obvious in his complete mastery of the spirits of evil. At any rate Simon and Peter followed Jesus at once, no doubt wondering very much what it all meant and what to become 'fishers of men' would entail. We can reasonably assume that Jesus made his choices after much prayer and thought. Here he is obviously choosing men who by the nature of their craft are brave, patient and enduring. We may fairly guess that their lives were comparatively simple and uncontaminated by the complications of city life. But that does not mean that they were 'simple' in the sense of being stupid.

Now we find Jesus calling James and John, the sons of Zebedee, in the same direct fashion. They, too, felt the authority behind his words, and promptly left both their business and their own father.

Jesus begins healing the sick

vs 21–34 They arrived at Capernaum, and on the Sabbath day Jesus walked straight into the synagogue and began teaching. They were amazed at his way of teaching, for he taught with the ring of authority – quite unlike the scribes. All at once, a man in the grip of an evil spirit appeared in the synagogue shouting out,

'What have you got to do with us, Jesus from Nazareth? Have you come to kill us? I know who you are – you're God's holy one!'

But Jesus cut him short and spoke sharply,

'Hold your tongue and get out of him!'

At this the evil spirit convulsed the man, let out a loud scream and left him. Everyone present was so astounded that people kept saying to each other,

'What on earth has happened? This new teaching has authority behind it. Why, he even gives his orders to evil spirits and they obey him!'

And his reputation spread like wild-fire through the whole Galilean district.

Then he got up and went straight from the synagogue to the house of Simon and Andrew, accompanied by James and John. Simon's mother-in-law was in bed with a high fever, and they lost no time in telling Jesus about her. He went up to her, took her hand and helped her to her feet. The fever left her, and she began to see to their needs.

Late that evening, after sunset, they kept bringing to him all who were sick or troubled by evil spirits. The whole population of the town gathered round the doorway. And he healed great numbers of people who were suffering from various forms of disease. In many cases he expelled evil spirits; but he would not allow them to say a word, for they knew perfectly well who he was.

Now we have the authority exhibited more publicly. We simply do not know whether Jesus was known by sight or repute in the lakeside town of Capernaum. The Sabbath day services in the synagogue were not very like our own Church services but they would certainly include a reading of the Law and the Prophets and some scribe who had better knowledge of the subject than the ordinary run of people, would interpret these to the congregation. No doubt on special occasions a visiting scribe, or expert in the Law, would be invited to give an exposition or message. But here Jesus, apparently on his own initiative, took over the teaching on that particular day. We may wonder a little at the amazement of the people, but we can make an intelligent guess at the reason for it. There is a world of difference between a man who gives a more or less routine exposition and a man who speaks with authority, the expert speaking on his own subject. This authoritative note produced excitement but it also provoked hostility. The man who suddenly shouted out may have been 'in the grip of an evil spirit' for many years, but it was the provocative quality of sheer goodness which inflamed the spirit of evil to reveal its implacable fury against Jesus. There, and in other places, Mark is at pains to point out that various spirits of evil recognize the power of Jesus immediately. It is as though latent evil is bound to show its hostility and its near-panic in the presence of sheer goodness. Today, in our cleverness, nearly all of us

On the evening of that day, he said to them, 'Let us cross over to the other side of the lake.' (Mark 4:35)

reject entirely the idea of possession by 'evil spirits'. All can be explained by psychology, by chemical faults in the body affecting the behaviour of the brain, or by personality deficiency, etc. It is arguable whether we are really much wiser than the men of nineteen hundred years ago. Certainly not all evil that is manifested in human life is to be explained by the power of evil spirits. Marvellous personality cures are made by psychological and even by chemical means. But the deep-set evil which spoils our common life cannot easily be explained away in modern 'scientific' terms. It is surely worth our thought and discussion, in studying Mark's record to see whether there could be any truth in the idea that there really are evil spirits which can invade the human spirit. There are men of high intelligence who believe firmly in the existence of evil spirits and have unshakeable evidence to prove both the condition of spirit-possession and its cure.

It is interesting that the evil spirit should have instantly recognized the intrinsic danger of the presence of Jesus. We might compare 1 John 3:8 where one of the main purposes of the coming of the Messiah is said to be 'to destroy the works of the devil'.

The title holy one of God is not a usual one in the New Testament; in fact it only occurs again in John 6:69. But there is no need to quibble about the use of titles; the point Mark is concerned to make is that evil recognizes the fatal force of good, even though Jesus had not as yet shown his hand. Despite its boastfulness and pride evil knows that it has no future. The end is inevitable, and the acute danger from goodness is sensed and expressed by fury.

Jesus has no wish to hear more from the spirits of evil, even though they were testifying to his own position as Messiah or Christ. His concern is with the well-being of the man possessed. Thus he speaks in sharp rebuke and, if we take the Greek word literally, tells the evil spirit to 'be muzzled'. It is not a polite expression and I must say I was tempted to translate it by the modern slang 'belt up'! The evil spirit gives a last

Then he left that district and came into his own
native town [Nazareth]. (Mark 6:1)

desperate expression of his power in the scream and the convulsion, and then goes. The crowds are absolutely amazed,
not merely at the new teaching, but at the hard-hitting
authority which accompanies it. No doubt exorcists of a kind
practised sporadically and with elaborate ritual from time to
time in their country. But a clear-cut confrontation of good
with evil, with the latter publicly and ignominiously routed,
was something extraordinary and never to be forgotten.
(Incidentally, how much would we, although believing in the
ultimate triumph of good, give to see such a downright
demonstration!) Mark's terse comment about the spread of his
reputation is of course just what we would expect. In a small
community modern means of communication are little quicker
than ordinary word of mouth.

Once again Mark establishes a sense of pace. Almost at
once Jesus is confronted with another form of evil – the
physical dis-ease of the body shown outwardly by a soaring
temperature.

Jesus acts at once without ceremony. Simon's mother-in-
law is immediately healed, and without the slightest delay
steps back into her role of housewife-provider. How true to
life is this homely touch of Mark. We all know the type of
good woman who, once she is recovered from her illness,
requires no fussy convalescence, but without hesitation picks
up the threads of her life from where she had been forced to
set them down!

The late evening was the obvious time for crowds of such
people to come, or be brought to Jesus. The day's work was
done and the sick who had worked despite their disabilities
were free to come to him. Similarly those who were bedridden
or housebound had their friends, freed from toil at the ending
of the day, to bring them to Jesus. Mark makes a distinction
between the sick and those who were troubled by evil spirits.
There is no reason to suppose that he is exaggerating when he
talks of the whole population being 'gathered round the doorway'. Capernaum was not a very large town even though it

had ambitions as a popular lakeside resort (see Matthew 11:23). Indeed with the story of what had happened earlier in the day ringing in their ears it would be well-nigh incredible if the whole population had not flocked to Jesus as soon as opportunity offered. This time Jesus will not allow the evil spirits, whom he had commanded to come out, to speak at all. We may make of this what we will, but it is obvious that Jesus did not want his cause advanced by the testimony of devils.

He retires for private prayer

vs 35–39 Then, in the early morning, while it was still dark, Jesus got up, left the house and went off to a deserted place, and there he prayed. Simon and his companions went in search of him, and when they found him, they said,

'Everyone is looking for you.'

'Then we will go somewhere else, to the neighbouring towns,' he replied, 'so that I may give my message there too – that is why I have come.'

So he continued preaching in their synagogues and expelling evil spirits throughout the whole of Galilee.

The days had already begun to be more than busy, and the demands on Jesus' time and energy almost too much to be borne. Thus Jesus can only find peace and quiet in the darkness of early morning in 'a deserted place'. The word used to describe such a place is certainly the same word as that used to describe the desert proper. But here it means a place where, through lack of water and pasture, not even a shepherd-boy would be found. It would be impertinent for us, even in imagination, to construct a possible time-scheme for Jesus' prayer activities at these times of withdrawal. But certainly we can guess that he renewed his contract with his Father, replenished his own spiritual reserves and prayed for the strength necessary for the tasks which lay ahead. The only way for a man upon whom great demands are made to retain his poise (and indeed his mental health) was, and is, to be still before God and be both open to his strength and flexible to his direction. Simon and his companions might well be thought to have been in a mild panic, at the unexplained disappearance of Jesus. The word to describe the search is a strong one, meaning almost 'pursued him'.

Here we can see the self-possession and poise of Jesus. The obvious and natural reaction which most of us would produce when told that everyone was looking for us would be to go back and meet them and do what we could to satisfy their needs. Jesus' reaction was the opposite. The fact that everyone was looking for him in one place was to him a certain sign that he must go somewhere else. The message must be spread as widely as possible. Therefore he now embarks on a preaching tour throughout Galilee, working through the probably large number of local synagogues. This ministry was as before – a matter of teaching and preaching and expelling evil spirits.

Jesus cures leprosy

vs 40–45 Then a leper came to Jesus, knelt in front of him and appealed to him,

'If you want to, you can make me clean.'

Jesus was filled with pity for him, and stretched out his hand and placed it on the leper, saying,

'Of course I want to – *be clean* !'

At once the leprosy left him and he was quite clean. Jesus sent him away there and then with the strict injunction,

'Mind you say nothing at all to anybody. Go straight off and show yourself to the priest, and make the offerings for your cleansing which Moses prescribed, as public proof of your recovery.'

But he went off and began to talk a great deal about

it in public, spreading his story far and wide. Consequently, it became impossible for Jesus to show his face in the towns and he had to stay outside in lonely places. Yet the people still came to him from all quarters.

It is difficult for us to understand what horror and revulsion the disease of leprosy caused among the people in those days. To some extent the horror persists. I can remember living within a mile or so of a leper colony in this country and can still recollect the difficulty the nurses and doctors had in getting ordinary people, such as shopkeepers and taxi-drivers, to have the remotest contact with the patients. These people, under modern care, had the disease under control and were now in the course of being cured. They were neither loathsome to look at nor repellent in their habits, nor were they in any way infectious, yet the centuries-old fear of leprosy persisted. However in those far-off days there were good reasons for men to be repelled as well as thoroughly frightened. The untreated leper had no man to care for him and no drugs or medicaments to deal with his condition. Thus his repulsive skin eruptions, his scars and mutilations were enough to revolt the stoutest heart, quite apart from the very severe view of the disease taken by the Jewish Law itself.

This leper was plainly desperate for recovery, and it does not take much imagination to see the psychological state that a lifetime of being shunned by his fellow-men would produce in a man's personality. He had become something less than a has over disease. The concentrated health of every part of his need. But Jesus, though he certainly must have been taught the various Jewish laws of 'uncleanliness', was not only filled with pity but took the unheard of step of actually stretching out his hand and touching him. Again we are met with this sense of authority, this time the command which wholeness has over disease. The concentrated health of every part of his being gave Jesus the power to order the disease to leave the man. And it did, completely.

A great deal has been written about what particular form of leprosy afflicted this unfortunate man. There are seven distinct varieties of the disease mentioned in Leviticus 13. Several modern scholars have suggested that it was not a true leprosy at all but a singularly repulsive skin condition such as psoriasis. Speculation is unhelpful here, for Jesus by his action, as well as by his subsequent instruction, recognizes the disease as some form of leprosy. Jesus was a faithful Jew and it was natural for him to order the man to exhibit himself to the priest and make the appropriate offerings for his cleansing as prescribed by the Law. This not only guaranteed that the cure had been effectual; it was, as Jesus said, a 'public proof' of the man's recovery. Some scholars seem to find a difficulty here. They cannot see why Jesus should on the one hand tell the man to keep his mouth shut and at the same time require him to give public evidence of his recovery. I cannot myself see the difficulty. Jesus most emphatically did not want himself known primarily as a wonder-worker and he knew how very difficult it is for a man who has been healed of a horrible disease to keep quiet about it. Yet, since the cure was real there was surely nothing inconsistent in following the normal practice of the Law and exhibiting proof that the miracle was genuine. But, as we might have guessed, the warnings of Jesus went unheeded. The man's perfectly understandable loquacity worked, as Jesus knew it would, to the disadvantage of his plans. The healing of leprosy was such a spectacular and almost unheard-of event that Jesus could no longer show himself in any of the towns. It was the lonely desert places for him again, although this time for a different reason. Yet even here nothing would stop people coming to him from all parts of the countryside.

CHAPTER TWO

*

Faith at Capernaum

vs 1–13 When he re-entered Capernaum some days later, a rumour spread that he was in somebody's house. Such a large crowd collected that while he was giving them his message it was impossible even to get near the doorway. Meanwhile, a group of people arrived to see him, bringing with them a paralytic whom four of them were carrying. And when they found it was impossible to get near him because of the crowd, they removed the tiles from the roof over Jesus' head and let down the paralytics's bed through the opening. And when Jesus saw their faith, he said to the man who was paralysed,

'My son, your sins are forgiven.'

But some of the scribes were sitting there silently asking themselves,

'Why does this man talk such blasphemy? Who can forgive sins but God alone?'

Jesus realized instantly what they were thinking, and said to them,

'Why must you argue like this in your minds? Which do you suppose is easier – to say to a paralysed man, "Your sins are forgiven", or "Get up, pick up your bed and walk"? But to prove to you that the Son of Man has full authority to forgive sins on earth, I say to you,' – and here he spoke to the paralytic – 'Get up, pick up your bed and go home.'

At once the man sprang to his feet, picked up his bed and walked off in full view of them all. Everyone was amazed, praised God and said,

35

'We have never seen anything like this before.'

Then Jesus went out again by the lake-side and the whole crowd came to him, and he continued to teach them.

The point is, naturally, that the healer and preacher has returned from the deserted places; he is *indoors*. The resultant crowd was what Jesus anticipated. No doubt he had his reasons for leaving the wilds; it is not surely fanciful to suggest that he was 'led' to this house for a critical and momentous event is to take place there.

Four friends bring their paralysed companion on a pallet or stretcher, but obviously there was no entrance at the door for a fit man, let alone a group of four, handicapped by carrying a fifth and helpless friend. Access to the roof of the house was common and easy. Most of these single-storied dwellings had flat roofs with an outside stairway leading to it. These four men (we naturally think of them as young and adventurous) were not only full of faith but determined and ingenious. We can easily imagine their reaction on meeting the impassable obstacle of sheer crowds at the doorway. 'No room for him through the door, lads? Then he'll have to go down through the roof.' We can imagine their half-humorous but completely determined remarks.

Literally: 'They de-roofed the roof.' The sort of house we are imagining here would have wooden rafters, not necessarily very strong for they have not much weight to bear. Over the timber could be laid rushes and earth, stones or tiles. At least we can be sure it was not a mere sun-blind or canopy! No, these determined men 'unroofed the roof'.

Jesus shows no surprise, although we can safely imagine that he smiled at this unusual and ingenious way of getting a sufferer to him. But he quickly and shrewdly notes *their* faith, and is able at once to declare the paralytic forgiven, and, in a few moments, healed. We know nothing of the paralytic's own faith or lack of it. He may well have been near despair, utterly depressed at the nature of his illness and crushed by a load of guilt. We do not, of course, know precisely what was causing the paralysis, but we do know that guilt was the underlying factor. Jesus knew by instinct, in a moment, what a modern psychiatrist might take months to discover, and even then find himself unable to help the patient to accept forgiveness. It *is* done, of course, and thank God for it, but it is worth noting that many of the 'miracles' of Jesus are in no sense 'magic'; they are infinitely speeded-up acts of normal healing. Faith seems to be the key to the unlocking of the formidable power of sheer goodness and wholeness. Today we may make the sufferer's burden heavier by urging him to 'have more faith'. It is we, those who care and love, upon whom the responsibility for 'faith' most probably rests. Do we pray 'in faith' with determination for those who suffer?

Here is Mark's first mention of the 'scribes' (v. 6). These men were trained in the knowledge and interpretation of the Law, and as such were honoured. They probably enjoyed 'front seats' in this small crowded house. Mark could not have *known* what the scribes were thinking, but he could naturally infer it.

Jesus, with his sensitivity and insight, knew what was going on in the scribes' minds immediately. It must at least have taken them aback to have their thoughts so accurately read. Jesus' words were blasphemy in their ears. He did not say, 'God will forgive you', or even 'has forgiven you', but 'Your sins are forgiven', thus plainly arrogating to himself a strictly divine function. They had no thought at all for the paralytic man.

Whether this splendid question (v. 9) was thought out by Jesus on the spur of the moment or whether he had meditated upon a situation which was bound to arise sooner or later, of course we cannot know. But it is a subtle, penetrating question and I can think of no single verbal riposte in any literature which comes within a mile of it. I believe it would do us good to see what fundamental issues this brilliant question raises.

(No, I am not going to list them : the reader must do his homework too!)

An end to guessing and argument, this the scribes shall *know*, and they cannot explain away what happens before their eyes. The note of authority is strong again here. We may imagine the sudden hush at the moment of instant healing. Then came the voices expressing amazement and certainly seeing the hand of God in this dramatic incident. They praised God, records Mark, and the next remark shows all the marks of authenticity. It is exactly what country-folk, or anyone else for that matter, would naturally say.

Jesus now goes into the open air and again to the shore of the lake. (At least here he cannot be surrounded on all sides!) The people flock after him and he continues his teaching, which had been interrupted. The teaching of which we have only the barest outline, even if we add all the Gospel narratives together, was always an integral part of Jesus' ministry. People are not usually changed fundamentally by healings or other demonstrations of power. They need to be taught – about God and life and themselves. They need to be reminded again and again that the kingdom of God (though rooted in Heaven) has invaded human life with the coming of God's Christ.

Jesus now calls 'a sinner' to follow him

vs 14–17 As Jesus went on his way, he saw Levi the son of Alphaeus sitting at his desk in the tax-office, and he said to him,

'Follow me!'

Levi got up and followed him. Later, when Jesus was sitting at dinner in Levi's house, a large number of tax-collectors and disreputable folk came in and joined him and his disciples. For there were many such people among his followers. When the scribes who were Pharisees saw him eating in the company of tax-collectors and outsiders, they remarked to his disciples,

'So he eats with tax-collectors and sinners!'

When Jesus heard this, he said to them,

'It is not the fit and flourishing who need the doctor, but those who are ill. I did not come to invite the "righteous", but the "sinners".'

The Romans made rich citizens responsible for the taxes which the Empire demanded. These 'solid citizens' would farm out the actual work of collecting the taxes to tax-collectors ('publicans' in the AV). The way was wide open for the unscrupulous and rapacious. Corruption was common and the tax-collector, quite apart from being in effect a Roman agent, was despised by most decent people.

It is out of this disreputable class that Jesus calls his next disciple, Levi. He leaves a busy desk, no doubt much unfinished business, and at once gets up and follows Jesus. In a sense Levi leaves more than Peter, Andrew, James and John. They could always, after all, return to fishing. But Levi is giving up a career, to which there could be no return. There can be little doubt that this Levi, the son of Alphaeus, is the same person as Matthew, later listed under this name in the list of the apostles (Mark 3:18).

It seems likely that this feast (Luke calls it 'a great feast') takes place in Matthew's own house. How natural for him to invite his former colleagues and others outside the social 'pale'.

'The scribes of the Pharisees', which is a literal translation of the Greek and appears in the 1881 Revised Version, does not make sense to me. We have no reason that I know of to think that a Pharisee had a staff or coterie of scribes, which is what such an expression would imply. But surely there was nothing to prevent a Pharisee from acquiring the specialized technical knowledge of the scribes. He might then be called 'a scribe from the Pharisees', or even 'a scribe who was a Pharisee'.

Another sharp double-edged comment from Jesus (v. 17). We can imagine the disdain with which the Pharisees, who prided themselves on being holy and separate, would view this motley rabble. The scribes, who prided themselves on their minute and exact knowledge of every facet of the Law, would share their contempt. Jesus' compressed verbal dart again could not fail to pierce the prideful armour of both groups. Are you so well yourselves, he says in effect, that you have no need of any further help? And if so, what should your attitude be towards those suffering – if they are sick, are you doing anything to heal them?

The word I have translated 'invite' means just that. It is the natural verb used when issuing invitations to a party or celebration. Jesus' 'party', in Matthew's house, was in no sense an exclusive get-together for those who knew they were well. His invitation was, and is, for those who know they are in need, know their own spiritual destitution and find life a weary and heavy business. It is not the man with protestations of his own goodness whom Jesus welcomes; it is those who know their need.

The question of fasting

vs 18–22 The disciples of John and the Pharisees were fasting. They came and said to Jesus,

'Why do those who follow John or the Pharisees keep fasts but your disciples do nothing of the kind?'

Jesus told them,

'Can you expect wedding-guests to fast in the bridegroom's presence? Fasting is out of the question as long as they have the bridegroom with them. But the day will come when the bridegroom will be taken away from them – that will be the time for them to fast.

'Nobody,' he continued, 'sews a patch of unshrunk cloth on to an old coat. If he does, the new patch tears away from the old and the hole is worse than ever. And nobody puts new wine into old wineskins. If he does, the new wine bursts the skins, the wine is spilt and the skins are ruined. No, new wine must go into new wine-skins.'

John's disciples, like many good Jews including the Pharisees, used fasting as part of their spiritual discipline. The Old Testament indeed approves of fasting on certain occasions, but by Jesus' time fasting had become so elaborate a ritual that the practice was almost defeating its own purpose. Any-way, Jesus reminds them of who he is, the centre of his followers' joy. You could as soon expect men to fast now that 'the bridegroom' is with them, as expect men to fast at a wedding-breakfast. But this time will end, and Jesus foresees, as most of his followers did not, that the time for sorrow and fasting would certainly come *when the bridegroom is taken away from them.*

Now listen, says Jesus in effect, something quite new has come into the world with me. Patching up old clothes or desperately stretching old leather wineskins will not cope with the new era which he brings with him. It is new, strong and dynamic. The gospel cannot be contained within any legal system; there is a freedom and explosive joy about it.

Jesus rebukes the sabbatarians

vs 23–28 One day he happened to be going through the cornfields on the Sabbath day. And his disciples, as they made their way along, began to pick the ears of corn. The Pharisees said to him,

'Look at that! Why should they do what is forbidden on the Sabbath day?'

Then he spoke to them.

'Have you never read what David did, when there was no food and he and his companions were famished? He went into the house of God when Abiathar was High

Priest, and ate the presentation loaves, which nobody is allowed to eat, except the priests – and even gave some of the bread to his companions? The Sabbath,' he continued, 'was made for man's sake; man was not made for the sake of the Sabbath. That is why the Son of Man is master even of the Sabbath.'

This is in itself a trivial incident. How ludicrous it is to compare the casual plucking of a few ears of corn with the hot dusty labour of reaping. But Jesus is determined to see that Man and the Law are seen in their proper perspective. He knew as well as they did that the hard labour of reaping was forbidden on the Sabbath (Exodus 24:21). But man was not made for the sake of the Sabbath – the Sabbath was meant to save men from the intolerable labour of a seven-day week. So Jesus takes the war into the enemies' camp. They want men to live by the Jewish Law and precedent, do they? All right then; suppose they consult their own precious Scriptures and see what David and his companions did when they were famished and no other food could be had but the twelve presentation loaves, kept in 'the house of meeting'. At this time it was merely a tent and the twelve loaves exhibited (which were renewed weekly) were a perpetual reminder of God's presence, particularly of God the provider.

Jesus rams home the lesson. The Sabbath is a thing, but man is a living soul. The Sabbath might serve man but it must never dominate him. The Son of Man (i.e. Representative Man or Man in the form which God wills for him) is master, even of the Sabbath.

(For the historically tidy-minded there is a little confusion here about Abiathar. In 1 Samuel 22:11 Ahimelech was high priest and Abiathar was one of his sons! The experts seem to agree that there is some confusion in the Hebrew text. Obviously Jesus and his hearers had grown familiar with the version favouring Abiathar.)

CHAPTER THREE

*

vs 1–6 On another occasion when he went into the
synagogue, there was a man there whose hand was
shrivelled, and they were watching Jesus closely to see
whether he would heal him on the Sabbath day, so that
they might bring a charge against him. Jesus said to the
man with the shrivelled hand,

'Stand up and come out here in front!'

Then he said to them,

'Is it right to do good on the Sabbath day, or to do
harm? Is it right to save life or to kill?'

There was a dead silence. Then Jesus, deeply hurt as
he sensed their inhumanity, looked round in anger at
the faces surrounding him, and said to the man,

'Stretch out your hand!'

And he stretched it out, and the hand was restored.
The Pharisees walked straight out and discussed with
Herod's party how they could get rid of Jesus.

This incident may have occurred on the following Sabbath
or perhaps, as Luke's version says, on 'another Sabbath'.
Commentators talk freely of the first three Gospel writers
'moving' this incident close to that of the plucking of corn.
I cannot think why they talk so confidently about the
Evangelists' 'moving' incidents about to form a pattern. It
seems to me much more likely that Jesus, who lived in close
touch with his Father, was following a divine plan. He is no
wandering preacher moving haphazardly around the countryside and stopping wherever he can collect a crowd. He moves

43

purposively as one who is dedicated to doing the will of him who sent him. Since this issue of the Sabbath was so fundamental, why should it not have been the deliberate choice of Jesus to act out once again, publicly and unforgettably, the principle that the Sabbath was made for man and not man for the Sabbath?

Almost certainly we are back in the Capernaum synagogue and those who were watching him had seen him at work before. According to the strict letter of the Law, relief from suffering could only be given on the Sabbath when life was actually in danger.

The man whose hand was shrivelled or withered was probably a conspicuous figure. Tradition has it that he was a worker in wood, but whatever his work he would be severely handicapped through some kind of muscular atrophy. It must have taken a good deal of courage for him to leave his seat and come and stand where all could see him clearly. Plainly Jesus speaks in the same authoritative voice that he has used before. He is obviously determined to make crystal clear the issue between the Law of taboos and prohibitions and the superior Law of love.

Another of Jesus' pointed and unanswerable questions occurs at v. 4. This one is unanswerable by the opponents of Jesus because they could not make the sensible answer without exploding their own legalistic and inhumane attitude. Mark alone records the complete hush that followed it. (Possibly it is a thing which Peter specially remembered and reported to Mark.) Jesus 'looked round'. To look round like this, with a quick searching glance, is an expression Mark uses some half a dozen times. Again it is probably a characteristic action vividly remembered by Peter and recounted to Mark.

Jesus was both hurt and angry. He was 'hurt' or possibly 'grieved' at their 'inhumanity', a word which means literally 'hardening of heart'. To the Hebrews the heart was the seat of thought rather than emotion, and it is this hardening of the normal processes of human thought, making them callous in their attitude towards the suffering of a fellow human being, which hurts Jesus so deeply. At the same time he feels anger, the righteous indignation of a good man against avoidable evil. This must have shown on Jesus' face as he looked round at them. Jesus gives the direct command and there is an instantaneous healing.

Apparently no one made any comment, nor even praised God for the good that had been done. All that Mark records is that the Pharisees stalked out as if in protest. That they should have consorted with the party of the Herodians points to a strange alliance indeed. As far as we know the Herodians were a political rather than a religious party with a strong pro-Roman flavour. Their antipathy to Jesus sprang from very different causes than that of the Pharisees, but deeply shared hatreds, one political and one religious, make strange bedfellows. Their intention was undoubtedly to kill him.

Jesus' enormous popularity

vs 7–12 Jesus now retired to the lake-side with his disciples. A huge crowd of people followed him, not only from Galilee, but from Judea and Idumea, some from the district beyond the Jordan and from the neighbourhood of Tyre and Sidon. This vast crowd came to him because they had heard about the sort of things he was doing. So Jesus told his disciples to have a small boat kept in readiness for him, in case the people should crowd him too closely. For he healed so many people that all those who were in pain kept pressing forward to touch him with their hands. Evil spirits, as soon as they saw him, acknowledged his authority and screamed,

'You are the Son of God!'

But he warned them repeatedly that they must not make him known.

Jesus, possibly sensing the threat to his life or at least to his liberty, now returns to the lake-side. The vast crowds which follow are by no means all 'locals'. People come not only from Galilee but from Jerusalem, Judea and Idumea in the south, from Perea in the east, and even as far away as the coastal district around Tyre and Sidon in the north-west.

The small boat was to be used more than once, and from now on takes the place of the speaker's position in the synagogue.

Even if Peter's recollection of the scene was a little exaggerated (and I don't see why it should have been), it is plain that very large crowds 'pressed forward to touch' (literally 'fell upon') the healer and master of 'evil' or 'unclean' spirits. Jesus again warns the healed (perhaps specially those whose evil spirits 'had recognized him') against advertising who he was. This was not the time, nor were these the men to proclaim Jesus' true mission. He did this either repeatedly or emphatically; the Greek does not give us a clear meaning.

Jesus chooses the twelve apostles

vs 13–19 Later he went up on to the hill-side and summoned the men whom he wanted, and they went up to him. He appointed a band of twelve to be his companions, whom he could send out to preach, with power to drive out evil spirits. These were the twelve he appointed :

Peter (which was the new name he gave Simon), James the son of Zebedee, and John his brother, (he gave them the name of Boanerges, which means the 'Thunderers'), Andrew, Philip, Bartholomew, Matthew, Thomas, James the son of Alphaeus, Thaddaeus, Simon the Patriot, and Judas Iscariot, who betrayed him.

Jesus goes up to the top of one of the hills above the lake. Luke says that Jesus spent all night in prayer before selecting

the Twelve. This is probably true, but possibly unknown to
Peter, Mark's 'source'. Jesus summons them and they come
to him.

I have translated the Greek into a 'band of twelve'.
Literally it is 'he made twelve', very satisfying in Greek,
implying that he brought into being a body of his own chosen
men to be with him and help him in his work. He empowers
these Twelve with the ability to proclaim the good news and
power to drive out evil spirits.

Peter was the new name Jesus gave to Simon. His name
was formally changed by Jesus when he suddenly blurted out
the truth about Jesus the Christ (see Matthew 16:18). This
new name (or its Hebrew equivalent Cephas) is used throughout the New Testament. Peter had been called by that name
for so many years in so many churches that it is quite natural
that he may not have mentioned to Mark how he became
Peter.

Boanerges is a nickname, probably used in jest to mark the
pair's sudden bursts of wrath (see Luke 9:54). The name is
not used again in the New Testament.

Jesus exposes an absurd accusation

vs 20–30 Then he went indoors, but again such a crowd
collected that it was impossible for them even to eat a
meal. When his relatives heard of this, they set out to
take charge of him, for people were saying, 'He must be
mad!'

The scribes who had come down from Jerusalem were
saying that he was possessed by Beelzebub, and that he
drove out devils because he was in league with the prince
of devils. So Jesus called them to him and spoke to them
in parables –

'How can Satan be the one who drives out Satan? If
a kingdom is divided against itself, then that kingdom

cannot last, and if a household is divided against itself, it cannot last either. And if Satan leads a rebellion against Satan then his ranks are split, he cannot survive and his end is near. No one can break into a strong man's house and steal his property, without first tying up the strong man hand and foot. But if he did that, he could ransack the whole house.

'Believe me, all men's sins can be forgiven and all their blasphemies. But there can never be any forgiveness for blasphemy against the Holy Spirit. That is an eternal sin.'

He said this because they were saying, 'He is in the power of an evil spirit.'

His 'relatives' or 'close friends'. No doubt their intention was admirable. Perhaps success had gone to Jesus' head; perhaps he had been driven out of his mind by the phenomenal strain that was being put upon him day after day. At least, they could take care of him and give him adequate rest and food.

Beelzebub is thought to mean the 'lord of flies'. Beelzebul, which is the better reading, is a difficult one. Some take it to mean 'the lord of filth', and others to mean 'the lord of the habitation', the master of the inhabited world and of the nether regions. Jesus obviously knew of this prince of evil, and he calls him by the popular name of 'Satan' or 'the evil one'. He also calls this evil power 'the Prince of this world' (John 12:31).

Jesus swiftly shows the absurdity of the scribes' suggestion that he is in league with the Devil. He also emphasizes the need for great spiritual power to enter Satan's domain and ruin it. This was obviously Jesus' role. See 1 John 3:8.

Many people worry, or used to worry, about the 'unforgivable sin'. God's mercy is great but even he is powerless to forgive the man who holds obstinately to his conviction that evil is right and good is wrong. Of course the man can repent or be converted and then be forgiven.

The scribes were in very great spiritual danger. By persuading themselves, and each other, that Jesus' work was done by evil power they are putting themselves in the position of the unforgivable. This blasphemy is an 'eternal sin', i.e. it persists beyond the present life of time and space. The scribes, despite their obduracy, must have heard these stern words of Jesus with some trepidation.

The new relationships in the kingdom

vs 31–35 Then his mother and his brothers arrived. They stood outside the house and sent a message asking him to come out to them. There was a crowd sitting round him when the message was brought telling him, 'Your mother and your brothers are outside looking for you.'

Jesus replied, 'And who are really my mother and my brothers?'

And he looked round at the faces of those sitting in a circle about him.

'Look!' he said, 'my mother and my brothers are here. Anyone who does the will of God is brother and sister and mother to me.'

Now the very heart of the family of Nazareth arrives, Mary his mother and his brothers. We cannot imagine Jesus as lacking in filial and family feeling. But he knows himself to be the Christ, saviour, husband, brother and friend to all the world. Agonizing as the decision must have been for him he knows that he must not be tied by the small loyalties of one earthly family. And so he demonstrates his universal relation to all who do God's will, publicly and unmistakably.

CHAPTER FOUR

*

The story of the sower

vs 1–20 Then once again he began to teach them by the lake-side. A bigger crowd than ever collected around him so that he got into the small boat on the lake and sat down, while the crowd covered the ground right down to the water's edge. He taught them a great deal in parables, and in the course of his teaching he said,

'Listen! A man once went out to sow his seed and as he sowed, some seed fell by the roadside and the birds came and gobbled it up. Some of the seed fell among the rocks where there was not much soil, and sprang up very quickly because there was no depth of earth. But when the sun rose it was scorched, and because it had no root, it withered away. And some of the seed fell among thorn-bushes and the thorns grew up and choked the life out of it, and it bore no crop. And there was some seed which fell on good soil, and when it sprang up and grew, pro-duced a crop which yielded thirty or sixty or even a hundred times as much as the seed.'

Then he added,

'Every man who has ears should use them!'

Then when they were by themselves, his close followers and the twelve asked him about the parables, and he told them.

'The secret of the kingdom of God has been given to you. But to those who do not know the secret, everything remains in parables, so that,

Seeing they may see, and not perceive;

and hearing they may hear, and not understand;

50

lest haply they should turn again, and it should be
forgiven them.'

Then he continued,

'Do you really not understand this parable? Then how
are you going to understand all the other parables? The
man who sows, sows the message. As for those who are
by the roadside where the message is sown, as soon as
they hear it Satan comes at once and takes away what
has been sown in their minds. Similarly, the seed sown
among the rocks represents those who hear the message
without hesitation and accept it joyfully. But they have
no real roots and do not last – when trouble or persecution arises because of the message, they give up their
faith at once. Then there are the seeds which were sown
among thorn-bushes. These are the people who hear the
message, but the worries of this world and the false
glamour of riches and all sorts of other ambitions creep
in and choke the life out of what they have heard, and
it produces no crop in their lives. As for the seed sown
on good soil, this means the men who hear the message
and accept it and do produce a crop – thirty, sixty, even
a hundred times as much as they received.'

In the peace and quiet of the lake-side Jesus' voice can be
heard by the crowds who throng the water-side. Mark says
that Jesus does a good deal of his teaching in parables and
here mentions two. We may wonder a little at the wisdom of
teaching in 'parables', but Jesus knew his hearers. A piece of
formal teaching is quickly forgotten, but a story which creates
a mental picture is much more easily retained in the mind
and can be meditated upon later.

We may wonder at the apparent wastefulness and ineffici-
ency of the sower in those days. One man broadcast the seed
from a shallow basket upon the extremely fertile earth. Later
it would be ploughed in with a primitive plough. But at the
first stage the seed was seriously at risk. Some would fall on

the path that bordered the field (there were no hedges). Some would fall on rocky patches where no depth of earth existed. Some would fall on 'thorny ground'. Such thorns are not like our thistles and we must think of it as land infested with the very common Arab weed *nabk*. When these weeds germinate they look very much like corn but eventually by their vigorous nature choke the life out of the latter.

Many of us who know this parable from childhood may still miss its main point. The word, or message of God, is not enforced upon men by sheer power nor are they compelled to believe by manifestations of healing or exorcism. No, the word of God, with all its intrinsic power of growth and reproduction, is sown in the hearts of men and is as vulnerable to loss or destruction as any earthly grain.

This warning of Jesus (v. 9) is meant to convey to his hearers that what he has just said contains a deep and serious truth. They are privileged to hear it but they also have the responsibility of thinking what it really means.

In a sense the Gospel of God is an open secret, but in another sense it remains a mystery. To those who are shallow or lazy or proud in mind the great truth of the Christian faith remain obscure or even nonsensical.

When people have allowed their minds to be influenced by worldly values they become blind to spiritual truths. Jesus quotes here Isaiah 6:10 and this is echoed in John 12:40, Acts 28:26. No one, I think, suggests that this blindness is incurable, but the New Testament affirms that it is common, and until it is removed the teaching of the death and resurrection of Jesus remains either a 'stumbling-block' or 'foolishness'. See 1 Corinthians 1:23.

The seed is the message of God and the parable simply shows how varied can be its reception. Some hear but the message never gets further than the ears. Some receive the message with enthusiasm, seeing it as good news, but they have no staying power, for they are not prepared to bear responsibility for it in the face of trouble or persecution. Then there are those who accept the word honestly enough but other things, what are nowadays called 'the pressures of contemporary life', and the ambition for comfortable affluence, literally choke the message to death. The affairs of this world now loom so large that the original impact of the word is completely lost. Lastly, there are the people who accept God's message deeply into their beings and, over the years, produce a splendid crop of what Paul calls the 'fruits of the Spirit' (Galatians 5:22).

This simple and memorable parable is familiar to anyone who preaches and teaches or otherwise communicates the message of the kingdom of God. We all know, from sad experience, that this is what happens when the message of God is preached and taught to men. It is a wry comfort that Jesus himself foresaw the vulnerability of the word as it is communicated. In a later parable we shall see the strength of the same word, but here Jesus the realist is giving a kindly warning.

Truth is meant to be used

vs 21–25 Then he said to them,

'Is a lamp brought into the room to be put under a bucket or underneath the bed? Surely its place is on the lamp-stand! There is nothing hidden which is not meant to be made perfectly plain one day, and there are no secrets which are not meant one day to be common knowledge. If a man has ears he should use them!

'Pay attention to what you hear,' he said to them. 'Whatever measure you use will be used towards you, and even more than that. For the man who has something will receive more. As for the man who has nothing, even his "nothing" will be taken away.'

The purpose of a lamp is to give light to its surroundings, not to keep light to itself. Jesus is surely hinting here that the light he is giving to his disciples is not meant to be a joyful secret kept merely among themselves but is to be used to illuminate the lives of others. Further, truth comes to expose what is secret or hidden, not to conceal and mystify.

These words about proper listening sound quite severe and are certainly meant to be taken seriously. Jesus is warning his disciples against careless listening, as well as recommending their full attention to whatever they hear him say. The reward for treasuring what one has heard is the gift of even more truth. The penalty for inattention, or careless listening, is that it becomes habitual, and it is possible for men to lose entirely their capacity for understanding spiritual truth.

Jesus gives pictures of the kingdom's growth

vs 26–34 Then he said,

'The kingdom of God is like a man scattering seed on the ground and then going to bed each night and getting up every morning, while the seed sprouts and grows up, though he has no idea how it happens. The earth produces a crop without any help from anyone: first a blade, then the ear of corn, then the full-grown grain in the ear. And as soon as the crop is ready, he sends the reapers in without delay, for the harvest-time has come.'

Then he continued,

'What can we say the kingdom of God is like? How shall we put it in a parable? It is like a tiny grain of mustard-seed which, when it is sown, is smaller than any seed that is ever sown. But after it is sown in the earth, it grows up and becomes bigger than any other plant. It shoots out great branches so that birds can come and nest in its shelter.'

So he taught them his message with many parables like these, as far as their minds could understand it. He did

not speak to them at all without using parables, although
in private he explained everything to his disciples.

As distinct from the vulnerability of the seed at the sowing
stage, Jesus now uses an analogy from farming to show the
strength inherent in the same seed. The farmer does his job
in preparing the ground for sowing, but the earth produces
a crop from the seed by a process for which the farmer is not
responsible and which he certainly does not understand. So
with the power of the word of God. It has this potential for
good and grows by a process which is in itself a mystery.
Jesus now emphasizes the power of the word with another
homely parable. The mustard-seed was well known for its
tiny size, but it could grow into a small tree, or large bush.
Here Jesus is encouraging his disciples to see that though
the initial reception of the word of God may seem small
to the point of insignificance, its power of growth is
enormous.

The method of teaching by parables was not, of course, the
invention of Jesus. To put a truth in pictorial or anecdotal
form had been used many times before. We simply do not
know why Jesus chose this particular way of imparting his
teaching nor do we know why he explained every parable to
his disciples afterwards.

Jesus shows himself master of natural forces

vs 35–41 On the evening of that day, he said to them,
          'Let us cross over to the other side of the lake.'
So they sent the crowd home and took him with them
in the small boat in which he had been sitting, accompanied by other small craft. Then came a violent squall
of wind which drove the waves aboard the boat until it
was almost swamped. Jesus was in the stern asleep on the
cushion. They awoke him with the words,
          'Master, don't you care that we're drowning?'

And he woke up, rebuked the wind, and said to the
waves,

'Hush now! be still!'

The wind dropped and there was a dead calm.

'Why are you so frightened? Do you not trust me even
yet?' he asked them.

But sheer awe swept over them, and they kept saying
to each other,

'Who ever can he be? – even the wind and the waves
do what he tells them!'

Mark is sure that Jesus made the crossing of the lake on the
same day and why should he not be right? Jesus had probably
had a most exhausting day teaching, explaining and answer-
ing questions. Apparently without going ashore he suggests
that they cross over to the other side of the lake to get some
needed rest and refreshment. The presence of the 'other small
craft' is only mentioned by Mark and again sounds like a
personal recollection of Peter.

These violent squalls can come down upon a lake which is
deep-set among the hills suddenly and with terrifying ferocity.
(I can personally recall this happening to me when in a
small boat in the middle of a loch set amid the hills of Skye.)
Jesus, in his great fatigue, is so deeply asleep that he apparently does not even notice the storm. The 'cushion' was either
a pillow or simply the leather seat normally occupied by the
steersman.

The note of reproach in the remark with which they wake
him is again peculiar to Mark, possibly once again due to the
acute memory of Peter. Jesus 'rebukes' the wind as though it
were some great beast that was getting out of control. He
speaks with the same authority which he used when commanding evil spirits. His command is obeyed instantly and a
dead calm ensues. Jesus' reproval in his question to the
disciples may strike us as extraordinary. Were they really
meant to trust him in a boat on the point of sinking while he

himself was fast asleep? Well, apparently they were, and now
the fear of drowning is replaced by a different kind of fear
altogether – sheer awe at the power of the man who can
control wind and waves.

As good Jews the disciples would no doubt remember the
Psalm (107:29) in which it is said that God 'maketh the storm
calm, so that the waves thereof are still'. Who then can this
man possibly be?

CHAPTER FIVE

*

Jesus meets a violent lunatic

vs 1–20 So they arrived on the other side of the lake in
the country of the Gerasenes. As Jesus was getting out of
the boat, a man in the grip of an evil spirit rushed out
to meet him from among the tombs where he was living.
It was no longer possible for any human being to restrain
him even with a chain. Indeed he had frequently been
secured with fetters and lengths of chain, but he had
simply snapped the chains and broken the fetters in
pieces. No one could do anything with him. All through
the night as well as in the day-time he screamed among
the tombs and on the hill-side, and cut himself with
stones. Now, as soon as he saw Jesus in the distance, he
ran and knelt before him, yelling at the top of his voice,

'What have you got to do with me, Jesus, Son of the
Most High God? For God's sake, don't torture me!'

For Jesus had already said, 'Come out of this man,
you evil spirit!'

Then he asked him,

'What is your name?'

'My name is legion,' he replied, 'for there are many of us.'

Then he begged and prayed him not to send 'them' out of the country.

A large herd of pigs was grazing there on the hill-side, and the evil spirits implored him, 'Send us over to the pigs and we'll get into them!'

So Jesus allowed them to do this, and they came out of the man, and made off and went into the pigs. The whole herd of about two thousand stampeded down the cliff into the lake and was drowned. The swineherds took to their heels and spread their story in the city and all over the countryside. Then the people came to see what had happened. As they approached Jesus, they saw the man who had been devil-possessed sitting there properly clothed and perfectly sane – the same man who had been possessed by 'legion' – and they were really frightened. Those who had seen the incident told them what had happened to the devil-possessed man and about the disaster to the pigs. Then they began to implore Jesus to leave their district. As he was embarking on the small boat, the man who had been possessed begged that he might go with him. But Jesus would not allow this.

'Go home to your own people,' he told him, 'and tell them what the Lord has done for you, and how kind he has been to you!'

So the man went off and began to spread throughout the Ten Towns the story of what Jesus had done for him. And they were all simply amazed.

In crossing to the other side of the lake Jesus moves into definitely Gentile territory. Gerasa was one of a league of Ten Towns (Decapolis) which though obedient to Rome were organized more like the city-states of Greece. He does not, however, find the rest and quiet that he must have needed for he is immediately confronted by a dangerous lunatic. The man who is 'possessed' has superhuman strength, and since it was impossible to restrain him he was probably driven out of the city and lived, as we might say, in the cemetery. Somehow it makes the possessed man all the more sinister because he spent his days and nights among the tombs and cut himself with stones.

Once again we have the fact of evil spirits instantly recognizing who Jesus is. This time, however, Jesus is called not by any Hebrew title but by a Greek one, 'Son of the Most High God'. Jesus had already commanded the evil spirit to come out and only when it cried for mercy did he ask its name. The reply is astonishing but it is not meant to be taken literally, for a legion could consist of more than 6000 soldiers. But no doubt to the victim of terrible internal conflicts there seemed to be an invasion by a great many alien personalities. We simply do not know why the unhappy man implored Jesus not to send 'them' out of the country. At any rate there was a large herd of pigs grazing nearby, a thing which would of course be impossible in Jewish territory, and the evil spirits ask to be sent into them. Whether this actually happened or whether the maniacal cries of the tormented man in his last convulsions stampeded the pigs we do not know. All we know is the fact that the 2000 pigs plunged down the cliff into the lake and were drowned.

The reaction to this happening is not quite what we would have expected. The people of Gerasa, having heard the swineherd's story, come out to see for themselves. What they see is the man who had been the terror and despair of the district properly clothed and obviously sane. The exercise of such tremendous power of exorcism, not to speak of the loss of 2000 pigs, is too much for them. 'They were really frightened', and implored Jesus to leave the district.

The man who had been cured of this terrible possession by evil spirits very naturally begged that he might join the men who were with Jesus. But this is no part of Jesus' plan. He tells the man kindly, but no doubt firmly, to go and tell the story of his wonderful cure to his own people. This he apparently did so that the whole Ten Towns district was filled with amazement.

Faith is followed by healing

vs 21–43 When Jesus had crossed again in the boat to the other side of the lake, a great crowd collected around him as he stood on the shore. Then came a man called Jairus, one of the synagogue presidents. And when he saw Jesus, he knelt before him, pleading desperately for his help.

'My little girl is dying,' he said. 'Will you come and put your hands on her – then she will get better and live.'

Jesus went off with him, followed by a large crowd jostling at his elbow. Among them was a woman who had suffered from haemorrhages for twelve years and who had gone through a great deal at the hands of many doctors, spending all her money in the process. She had derived no benefit from them but, on the contrary, was getting worse. This woman had heard about Jesus and came up behind him under cover of the crowd, and touched his cloak.

'For if I can only touch his clothes,' she kept saying, 'I shall be all right.'

The haemorrhage was stopped immediately, and she knew in herself that she was cured of her trouble. At once Jesus knew intuitively that power had gone out of him, and he turned round in the middle of the crowd and said,

'Who touched my clothes?'

His disciples replied,

'You can see this crowd jostling you. How can you ask, "Who touched me?" '

But he looked all round at their faces to see who had done so. Then the woman, scared and shaking all over because she knew that she was the one to whom this thing had happened, came and flung herself before him and told him the whole story. But he said to her,

'Daughter, it is your faith that has healed you. Go home in peace, and be free from your trouble.'

While he was still speaking, messengers arrived from the synagogue president's house, saying,

'Your daughter is dead – there is no need to bother the master any further.'

But when Jesus heard this message, he said to the president of the synagogue,

'Now don't be afraid, just go on believing!'

Then he allowed no one to follow him except Peter and James and John, James' brother. They arrived at the president's house and Jesus noticed the hubbub and all the weeping and wailing, and as he went in, he said to the people in the house,

'Why are you making such a noise with your crying? The child is not dead; she is fast asleep.'

They greeted this with a scornful laugh. But Jesus turned them all out, and taking only the father and mother and his own companions with him, went into the room where the child was. Then he took the little girl's hand and said to her in Aramaic,

'Little girl, I tell you to get up!'

At once she jumped to her feet and walked round the room, for she was twelve years old. This sight sent the others nearly out of their minds with joy. But Jesus gave them strict instructions not to let anyone know what had happened – and ordered food to be given to the little girl.

Jesus returns to the western side of the lake and is met immediately by a huge crowd. Out of this crowd comes a man, Jairus, a synagogue president. He would be the man responsible for the order and worship as well as the upkeep of the local synagogue. He is obviously already completely convinced that Jesus can heal and begs for his help. Luke tells us that Jairus' daughter was his only one and Mark does not. Nevertheless the words I have translated 'my little girl' are a form of endearment found only in Mark and may imply a particularly close relationship such as a father might have for his only daughter.

Between this desperate appeal from Jairus and Jesus' arrival at his house comes the oddly moving incident of the woman who suffered from a chronic haemorrhage. Frail and desperate she may be but she is absolutely determined to touch, at any rate, the clothes of Jesus. Despite the milling crowd she manages to achieve this touch made in faith. Jesus senses this, and absurd though it seems to the disciples that he should ask such a question amid the jostling throng, he asks who touched his clothes. Terrified at the publicity and possibly scared at her own audacity, the woman comes forward in fear and trembling. She tells her pitiful story in full for every-body to hear. Jesus speaks to her with the deepest compassion. No one else is called 'daughter'. But he assures the woman that it is her faith in him that has saved her. It is perhaps worth noting that the miracles of healing recorded by Mark are always associated with faith. They are no mere haphazard demonstrations of power.

Now comes further drama. Messengers arrive from Jairus' house saying that his daughter is dead and there is no need to trouble the master any further. Jesus is not at all perturbed by this, and turning to Jairus, he tells him not to be afraid but simply to keep on believing. It must have taken some force of character as well as some authority to whittle the crowd down to just a few chosen disciples as they approached the synagogue president's house. It was considered a duty for the women of the house, as soon as a death had occurred, to announce their grief by noisy wailing and lamentation, not infrequently assisted by doleful music from professional mourners who naturally would be standing by.

Again we note the authority of Jesus. He declares as a fact

that the child is not dead but fast asleep. Now this does not mean that Jesus thought of her as being in some kind of coma. 'Sleeping' was a common euphemism for dying and is used so several times in the New Testament, e.g. John 11:11, 1 Corinthians 15:7. The crowd of mourners greets Jesus' words with derision. At this Jesus turns them out and leaves himself with the parents of the child and his three chosen followers. Then, speaking his native Aramaic, he takes the little girl's hand and tells her to get up. The miracle happens at once and the little girl begins to walk around, for she is no infant, she is twelve years old. Although Jesus believed that he had raised the little girl literally from death and not merely raised her out of a coma, he does not want this power of his known yet. Hence the strict injunction to keep the matter to themselves, and the commonsensical order to give the little girl something to eat!

CHAPTER SIX

*

The 'prophet without honour'

vs 1–6 Then he left that district and came into his own native town, followed by his disciples. When the Sabbath day came, he began to teach in the synagogue. The congregation were astonished at what they heard, and remarked,

'Where does he get all this? What is this wisdom that he has been given – and what about these marvellous things that he can do? He's only the carpenter, Mary's son, the brother of James, Joses, Judas and Simon; and his sisters are living here with us!'

And they were deeply offended with him. But Jesus said to them,

'No prophet goes unhonoured – except in his native town or with his own relations or in his own home!'

And he could do nothing miraculous there apart from laying his hands on a few sick people and healing them; their lack of faith astonished him.

Jesus now leaves Jairus' house and proceeds to his own native town of Nazareth where he grew up and plied his trade as a carpenter. Matthew recounts such a visit and so does Luke; much ingenuity has been spent in the attempt to harmonize the three accounts, but there is no reason to suppose that Jesus visited his home town only once. It may well be that the visit described in Luke 4, which ended in a murderous attempt on Jesus' life, was his final one.

Once more Jesus speaks in a synagogue on the Sabbath, this time to a congregation composed of those who had known him all his life. They had seen him grow up, seen him doing his work as a carpenter and his brothers and sisters were still living amongst them. We can easily imagine their astonishment at the authority and power of Jesus' words, and they were well aware of his reputation as a healer.

It is almost impossible to translate the Greek word which I have translated 'they were deeply offended with him.' The word is *eskandalizonto*, but to say that they were 'scandalized' by him does not convey the proper meaning in today's English. *Skandalon*, the noun from which the verb is derived, means something which trips a man up, or snares him in a trap. Thus it came to mean to cause offence or to entice a person into a wrong way of thinking. It is thus used in the Greek version of the Old Testament. Perhaps we can get fairly near the meaning if we imagine the scene. Jesus' old familiar friends would be asking, 'Who does he think he is?' and would be outraged at his apparent presumption. They knew perfectly well that he had had no special instruction or training. At the same time they could not deny the authority and truth of what he was teaching and they were therefore baffled as well. Probably there is no single English word which we can use in translation, but we might spare a little imaginative sympathy for all the ordinary God-fearing people who suddenly find Jesus the carpenter speaking with such power and wisdom. The proverb about the 'prophet being without honour' was common in the ancient world and Jesus gives a slight twist to apply it to the situation in which he finds himself.

As we have noted before, healing only occurs in Mark's accounts in response to faith. Here, where there is very little faith, very little healing takes place. The real humanity of Jesus is shown by the fact that certain things could 'astonish' him. If he had merely been God pretending to be man there could have been no such thing as astonishment.

The twelve are sent out to preach the gospel

vs 7–13 Then he made his way round the villages, continuing his teaching. He summoned the twelve, and began to send them out in twos, giving them power over evil spirits. He instructed them to take nothing for the road except a staff – no bread, no satchel and no money in their pockets. They were to wear sandals and not to take more than one coat. And he told them,

'Wherever you are, when you go into a house, stay there until you leave that place. And wherever people will not welcome you or listen to what you have to say, leave them and shake the dust off your feet as a protest against them!'

So they went out and preached publicly that men should change their whole outlook. They expelled many evil spirits and anointed many sick people with oil and healed them.

Jesus now embarks on a teaching tour of the surrounding villages, and to help him he sends out the Twelve with the simplest possible equipment physically speaking, but spiritually empowered to conquer evil spirits. This was in the nature of a 'commando' raid, for no time was to be lost in persuading the reluctant or pacifying the hostile. Jesus' plan seems to be at this point to spread the basic message of the Kingdom as widely as possible. The mission was by no means a total success.

Herod's guilty conscience

vs 14–29 All this came to the ears of king Herod, for Jesus' reputation was spreading, and people were saying that John the Baptist had risen from the dead, and that was why he was showing such miraculous powers. Others maintained that he was Elijah, and others that he was one of the prophets of the old days come back again. But when Herod heard of all this, he said,

'It must be John whom I beheaded, risen from the dead!'

For Herod himself had sent and arrested John and had him bound in prison, all on account of Herodias, wife of his brother Philip. He had married her, though John used to say to Herod, 'It is not right for you to possess your own brother's wife.' Herodias herself nursed a grudge against John for this and wanted to have him executed, but she could not do it, for Herod had a deep respect for John, knowing that he was a just and holy man, and kept him under his protection. He used to listen to him and be profoundly disturbed, and yet he enjoyed hearing him.

Then a good opportunity came, for Herod gave a birthday party for his courtiers and army commanders and for the leading people in Galilee. Herodias' daughter came in and danced, to the great delight of Herod and his guests. The king said to the girl,

'Ask me anything you like and I will give it to you!'

And he swore to her,

'I will give you whatever you ask me, up to half my kingdom!'

And she went out and spoke to her mother,

'What shall I ask for?'

And she said,

'The head of John the Baptist!'

The girl rushed back to the king's presence, and made her request.

'I want you to give me, this minute, the head of John the Baptist on a dish!' she said.

Herod was aghast, but because of his oath and the presence of his guests, he did not like to refuse her. So he sent the executioner straightaway to bring him John's head. He went off and beheaded him in the prison, brought back his head on the dish, and gave it to the girl who handed it to her mother. When his disciples heard what had happened, they came and took away his body and put it in a tomb.

This Herod was not really a king, but a tetrarch, i.e. a ruler over a quarter of a certain territory. But no doubt it was expedient to flatter his vanity and call him 'king'. He is Herod Antipas, one of the sons of the so-called Herod the Great, whose insane jealousy led to what we nowadays call the 'slaughter of the innocents'. Mark uses the fact that Herod had heard of the supernatural actions of Jesus and his close disciples to insert the story of the murder of John the Baptist. Herod, like many powerful tyrants of old, is intensely superstitious. His conscience is uneasy and when he hears of Jesus' 'mighty works' he jumps to the conclusion that this must be John whom he had beheaded, come back from the dead, a man whom in life he had respected and now returned from the dead he has every reason to fear. Mark briefly recalls the circumstances of this sordid story. Herod had divorced his first wife and she had departed to her father, King Aretas, who ruled over Arabia-Petrea. John had denounced the evil of this divorce and Herod's adulterous marriage to his brother Philip's wife. He suffered, as many had before and since, for boldly speaking the truth.

The apostles return: the huge crowds make rest impossible

vs 30–38 The apostles returned to Jesus and reported to him every detail of what they had done and taught.

'Now come along to some quiet place by yourselves, and rest for a little while,' said Jesus, for there were people coming and going incessantly so that they had not even time for meals. They went off in the boat to a quiet place by themselves, but a great many saw them go and recognized them, and people from all the towns hurried on foot to get there first. When Jesus disembarked he saw the large crowd and his heart was touched with pity for them because they seemed to him like sheep without a shepherd. And he settled down to teach them about many things. As the day wore on, his disciples came to him and said,

'We are right in the wilds here and it is getting late. Let them go now, so that they can buy themselves something to eat from the farms and villages around here.'

But Jesus replied,

'You give them something to eat!'

'You mean we're to go and spend twenty pounds on bread? Is that how you want us to feed them?'

'What bread have you got?' asked Jesus. 'Go and have a look.'

And when they had found out, they told him,

'We have five loaves and two fish.'

This is the first time Mark gives the title 'apostles' (meaning 'those who are sent') to the Twelve. No doubt some time had passed since, for example, the rubbing of the ears of corn which would be in the autumn and the present incident takes place in the spring. Although Jesus makes the highest demands he is no slave-driver. He quickly recognized the disciples' need for rest, and to get away in the small boat seemed the only escape from the clamorous crowds. However, in the event, they did not get much time for rest, for the crowds saw in which direction they were heading and hurried on foot to forestall them. This would not have been difficult, for unless conditions were extremely favourable to the small boat a man hurrying along on foot could travel more quickly even though the distance was greater. Jesus was probably making for some quiet place by the lake-side near Bethsaida, a matter of some four miles by water and considerably more by land.

The dominant emotion with many people at seeing the crowds awaiting their disembarkation would have been exasperation. 'Why can't they leave us alone for a bit so that we can rest and have time for a proper meal?' This would be a natural enough thought to have in the circumstances. But Jesus' great compassion is stronger than his sense of fatigue. He sees the people helpless and confused like 'sheep without a shepherd'. The idea of God or his representative being a shepherd to the souls of men comes from the Old Testament, but Jesus is plainly seeing the people's shepherdless state as sadly true at this moment. The priestly caste is giving them no spiritual leadership and the scribes, those experts in the Law, were simply laying further rules upon people's already overburdened backs. So Jesus begins to teach them about many things. We should naturally like to know more about these 'many things', but unless some fresh discovery is made of some ancient contemporary manuscript we have to be content with what we can learn from Matthew, Mark, Luke and John.

The time would be late in the day, and the miraculous feeding must have taken place before sunset. The disciples are themselves concerned about the crowds who have apparently rushed round to hear the words of Jesus without making any provision for their own nourishment. The sensible thing seems to them to dismiss the crowds and let them wander off to villages and hamlets not far away to buy food. Jesus staggers them, and indeed us, by commanding the disciples to feed the crowds themselves! The disciples make a hasty calculation and reckon they'd have to make an outlay of twenty pounds (this is a very rough equivalent of its value then; 200 silver denarii might well be worth much more today). But Jesus does not mean them to spend money even if they had as much as twenty pounds between them. He asks them to find out what are the total food resources available, to receive the reply that they had five loaves and two fish.

Jesus miraculously feeds five thousand people

vs 39–44 Then Jesus told them to arrange all the people in parties, sitting on the green grass. And they settled down, looking like flower-beds, in groups of fifty or a hundred. Then Jesus took the five loaves and the two fish, and looking up to Heaven, thanked God, broke the loaves and gave them to the disciples to distribute to the people. And he divided the two fish among them all. Everybody ate and was satisfied. Afterwards they collected twelve baskets full of pieces of bread and fish that were left over. There were five thousand men who ate the loaves.

Difficult as it may be to believe, this is a miracle that every Christian must come to terms with. It is not so much a question of 'is this possible?' for with God all things are possible, as 'would God have acted like this on such an occasion?' I think we can dismiss without ceremony the common 'explanation' that the production of the small picnic lunch worked on the consciences of the rest of the crowd so that they produced their previously concealed stocks of food. Even if this were so it could hardly have given rise to an exaggerated account subsequently to be regarded as a miracle. I believe that we must accept what Mark, drawing on Peter's memory, records.

Colour does not feature very largely in the Gospel stories and it is noteworthy here that the people sat down on the *green* grass. Further, after being arranged, by Jesus' order, in fifties and hundreds, they might well have presented the appearance of flower-beds of variegated colour. The first meaning of the Greek word *prasiai* is 'flower-beds', and this might easily have struck the observant eye of Peter as he helped with the orderly distribution of the miraculously multiplied food. There are those who would make *prasiai* mean 'herb-gardens', but this surely robs the incident of its vivid eye-witness appeal. Herb-gardens are green and there would be no eye-catching sight in rectangular patches of green on a green background. But the varied colours of cloaks and head-dresses of the people might easily have suggested the literal meaning of 'flower-beds'. I think we can also dismiss a theory once held that Jesus divided the five loaves and two fish into minute quantities so that each person had a 'token' meal, thus anticipating the eucharistic practice of the Church some years later. But not only does this seem physically highly unlikely for the portions would have been microscopic, but the Gospel accounts go out of their way not only to state that the people's appetites were fully satisfied, but that there were baskets full of scraps left over.

Nevertheless, the old lesson remains. If we give fully and freely to our Lord what little we have he is quite capable of multiplying its use to many thousands. Any writer, broadcaster or indeed preacher knows how true this is.

Jesus' mastery over natural law

vs 45–56 Directly after this, Jesus made his disciples get aboard the boat and go on ahead to Bethsaida on the other side of the lake, while he himself sent the crowds home. And when he had sent them all on their way, he

went off to the hill-side to pray. When it grew late, the
boat was in the middle of the lake, and he was by himself on land. He saw them straining at the oars, for the
wind was dead against them, and in the small hours he
went towards them, walking on the waters of the lake,
intending to come alongside. But when they saw him
walking on the water, they thought he was a ghost and
screamed out. For they all saw him and they were
absolutely terrified. But Jesus at once spoke quietly to
them,

'It's all right, it is I myself; don't be afraid!'

And he climbed aboard the boat with them, and the
wind dropped. But they were scared out of their wits.
They had not had the sense to learn the lesson of the
loaves; their minds were still in the dark.

And when they had crossed over to the other side of
the lake, they landed at Gennesaret and tied up there.
As soon as they came ashore, the people recognized Jesus
and rushed all over the countryside and began to carry
the sick around on their beds to wherever they heard he
was. Wherever he went, in villages or towns or hamlets,
they laid down their sick right in the market-places and
begged him that they might 'just touch the edge of his
cloak'. And all those who touched him were healed.

It has been suggested that the crowd who rushed round to
meet Jesus might have been the same crowd, mentioned in
John's Gospel, who saw in Jesus a born leader and wanted
to make him king. If this is so, Jesus acts with some firmness to
discourage the idea. He sends the disciples safely away in the
small boat while he himself goes up into the mountains to
pray.

Now it is the small hours of the night. Jesus, I must say I
feel quite naturally, walks towards them on the waters of the
lake. I am not convinced that he 'would have passed them
by'. The natural meaning of the Greek word *parerchomai*

(although of course it can mean 'pass by') would be to pass alongside, no doubt to help and encourage them in their strenuous rowing against the wind. It is difficult to see how this story arose unless it actually happened. We are dealing partly, at least, with seasoned fishermen who certainly wouldn't mistake a man paddling in the shallows for one actually walking on the water.

Naturally, since in their minds all solid bodies sink in water he must be some sort of apparition or ghost. Jesus reassures them, but Mark declares that even after witnessing the miracle of feeding a large number of people, they still do not seem to realize who Jesus is and what are his powers.

However, despite their awe, they welcome him aboard and as soon as they come ashore at Gennesaret they are besieged again by the needy crowds. The demand for Jesus' healing power seems to have been even more pronounced in the Gennesaret district.

CHAPTER SEVEN

*

Jesus exposes the danger of man-made traditions

vs 1–23 And now Jesus was approached by the Pharisees and some of the scribes who had come from Jerusalem. They had noticed that his disciples ate their meals with 'common' hands – meaning that they had not gone through a ceremonial washing. (The Pharisees, and indeed all the Jews, will never eat unless they have washed their hands in a particular way, following a traditional rule. And they will not eat anything bought in the market until they have first performed their 'sprinkling'. And there are many other things which they consider important, concerned with the washing of cups, jugs and basins.) So the Pharisees and the scribes put this question to Jesus,

'Why do your disciples refuse to follow the ancient tradition, and eat their bread with "common" hands?'

Jesus replied,

'You hypocrites, Isaiah described you beautifully when he wrote –

This people honoureth me with their lips,

But their heart is far from me.

But in vain do they worship me,

Teaching as doctrines the precepts of men.

You are so busy holding on to the traditions of men that you let go the commandment of God!'

Then he went on,

'It is wonderful to see how you can set aside the commandment of God to preserve your own tradition! For Moses said, "Honour thy father and thy mother" and "He that speaketh evil of father or mother, let him die the death." But you say, "If a man says to his father or his mother, Korban – meaning, I have given God whatever duty I owed to you", then he need not lift a finger any longer for his father or mother, so making the word of God impotent for the sake of the tradition which you hold. And this is typical of much of what you do.'

Then he called the crowd close to him again, and spoke to them,

'Listen to me now, all of you, and understand this. There is nothing outside a man which can enter into him and make him "common". It is the things which come out of a man that make him "common"!'

Later, when he had gone indoors away from the crowd, his disciples asked him about this parable.

'Oh, are you as dull as they are?' he said. 'Can't you see that anything that goes into a man from outside cannot make him "common" or unclean? You see, it doesn't go into his heart, but into his stomach, and passes out of the body altogether, so that all food is clean enough. But,' he went on, 'whatever comes out of a man, that is what makes a man "common" or unclean. For it is from inside, from men's hearts and minds, that evil thoughts arise – lust, theft, murder, adultery, greed, wickedness, deceit, sensuality, envy, slander, arrogance and folly! All these evil things come from inside a man and make him unclean!'

It is becoming increasingly obvious that Jesus' healing and teaching is arousing considerable hostility among the 'establishment' of his day. This party of Pharisees and scribes have plainly come down from Jerusalem with the idea of finding fault. Now it is over the matter of the ceremonial washing, which had become by Jesus' day quite an elaborate ritual. This was not in the interests of hygiene as we know it, since germs were unknown, but simply that their hands might have been defiled by something or someone in the market-place or elsewhere. This action, with the help of the 'elders', had developed into a strong tradition among the Pharisees and their friends.

Jesus, as usual, goes to the heart of the matter. Their traditions have produced an elaborate lip-service to God, but their hearts are as far from him as ever. They have indeed reached the unhappy state where 'the traditions of men' have become more important than 'the commandment of God'. Jesus uses an apt explanation which may have been common in his day. 'Korban' means dedicated to God, and apparently a man could vow that all his goods were so dedicated to God that he need not use them to 'honour his father and mother', which is the commandment of God. Such a vow was to all intents and purposes irrevocable. This is the bad side of tradition, as Jesus makes crystal clear.

Jesus now states an important principle (v. 15). We can be pretty sure that he was not against normal washing (see the story in Luke 7:36–50). But he is emphatic that the things

which really defile people are not the foodstuffs which go into
their mouths but the evil things which arise from their
imaginations. He had a perfect example before him here, for
the Pharisees and scribes were doubtless ceremonially faultless
but, as Jesus knows, there are already in their hearts such
things as malice, envy, spite and even the desire to kill.

The faith of a gentile is rewarded

vs 24–30 Then he got up and left that place and went
off to the neighbourhood of Tyre. There he went into a
house and wanted no one to know where he was. But it
proved impossible to remain hidden. For no sooner had
he got there, than a woman who had heard about him,
and who had a daughter possessed by an evil spirit,
arrived and prostrated herself before him. She was a
Greek, a Syrophoenician by birth, and she asked him to
drive the evil spirit out of her daughter. Jesus said to her,

'You must let the children have all they want first. It
is not right, you know, to take the children's food and
throw it to the dogs.'

But she replied,

'Yes, Lord, I know, but even the dogs under the table
eat the scraps the children leave.'

'If you can answer like that,' Jesus said to her, 'you
can go home! The evil spirit has left your daughter.'

And she went back to her home and found the child
lying quietly on her bed, and the evil spirit gone.

Jesus now goes north, presumably to get a measure of peace
and quiet, and moves into Gentile territory. No doubt his
reputation has preceded him, for his longed-for privacy was
invaded almost at once by the Syrophoenician woman.
Matthew calls her 'a woman of Canaan' which means that
she belonged to a race disowned by orthodox Jews. She was
also a Greek, which meant, of course, that she was a Gentile,

and she came from the Roman province of Syria. In short, Mark is suggesting that she is really an outsider. Jesus' basic mission was first to the Jews, as indeed was Paul's a few years later, and this he makes clear in his reply to the woman's request. Of course it is possible, indeed I think probable, that the remark was made with a smile and perhaps a twinkle in the eye, for in normal use the word 'dog' was a term of utter contempt. But the woman had quickness of wit as well as the conviction that Jesus could heal her daughter. Jesus recognizes both; it is the faith which enables him to assure her that she can go home and find her daughter perfectly well.

The probability is that Mark records this singular incident to show a) that the fame of Jesus had spread to the surrounding Gentile countryside and b) that Jesus' compassion embraced the needs of those who are not God's 'special children'.

Jesus restores speech and hearing

vs 31–37 Once more Jesus left the neighbourhood of Tyre and passed through Sidon towards the Lake of Galilee, and crossed the Ten Towns territory. They brought to him a man who was deaf and unable to speak intelligibly, and they implored him to put his hand upon him. Jesus took him away from the crowd by himself. He put his fingers in the man's ears and touched his tongue with his own saliva. Then looking up to Heaven, he gave a deep sigh and said to him in Aramaic,

'Open!'

And his ears were opened and immediately whatever had tied his tongue came loose and he spoke quite plainly. Jesus gave instructions that they should tell no one about this happening, but the more he told them, the more they broadcast the news. People were absolutely amazed, and kept saying,

'How wonderfully he has done everything! He even makes the deaf hear and the dumb speak.'

Jesus' return route looks extremely difficult on the map! There may have been a purpose in it of which we know nothing, or the geography of Mark, or possibly Peter, may have been inadequate. In the healing story of the deaf and virtually mute man there is no direct mention of faith on the sufferer's part, but it is difficult to see how a man who was stone-deaf and incapable of coherent speech could express his faith. In any case there must have been, as in the case of the man 'borne of four', considerable faith on the part of the men who brought him to Jesus. Jesus takes the man away from the crowd, but not so far that his actions were not observed. By putting his fingers into the man's ears and touching his tongue with his own saliva he is emphasizing his intention to heal. Then by the obvious sign of looking up to Heaven to indicate that healing comes from God, Jesus gives a deep 'sigh' or 'groan', probably indicating his profound sympathy with the man's condition and utters a short command in his native Aramaic. He orders the defective organs to 'be opened'. The use of his native tongue is another small touch remembered and treasured by Peter.

Once again after the act of healing Jesus repeats his warning that it should not be talked about, but in vain. It would appear that the same people who had implored him to leave the country (5:17) are now singing his praises.

CHAPTER EIGHT

*

He again feeds the people miraculously

vs 1–10 About this time it happened again that a large crowd collected and had nothing to eat. Jesus called his disciples over to him and said,

'My heart goes out to this crowd; they have been with me three days now and they have no food left. If I send them off home without anything, they will collapse on the way – and some of them have come from a distance.'

His disciples replied,

'Where could anyone find the food to feed them here in this deserted spot?'

'How many loaves have you got?' Jesus asked them.

'Seven,' they replied.

So Jesus told the crowd to settle themselves on the ground. Then he took the seven loaves into his hands, and with a prayer of thanksgiving broke them, and gave them to the disciples to distribute to the people; and this they did. They had a few small fish as well, and after blessing them, Jesus told his disciples to give these also to the people. They ate and they were satisfied. Moreover, they picked up seven baskets full of pieces left over. The people numbered about four thousand. Jesus sent them home, and then he boarded the boat at once with his disciples and went on to the district of Dalmanutha.

Here we have another hungry crowd fed. Some look upon this as a repetition or 'doublet' of the previous feeding. This is a polite way of saying that Mark is repeating himself. But it is surely unlikely that Mark putting together the shortest of the Gospels, would include any mere repetition. There is no good reason to suppose that Jesus did not repeat on many occasions his teaching, his parables, his acts of healing; and here repeats something which he had already done. There are differences in the numbers, in which some have found profound significance, but I do not think they need seriously concern us.

We do not know where Dalmanutha (v. 10) is, though several speculations have been made. All we know is that it is part of the lake-side area, since after a brief brush with the Pharisees, they take to the boat again.

Jesus refuses to give a sign

vs 11–21 Now the Pharisees came out and began an argument with him. They were out to test him and wanted a sign from Heaven. Jesus gave a deep sigh, and then said,

'What makes this generation want a sign? I can tell you this, they will certainly not be given one!'

Then he left them and got aboard the boat again, and crossed the lake.

The disciples had forgotten to take any food and had only one loaf with them in the boat. Jesus spoke seriously to them, 'Keep your eyes open! Be on your guard against the "yeast" of the Pharisees and the "yeast" of Herod!' And this sent them into an earnest consultation among themselves because they had brought no bread. Jesus knew it and said to them,

'Why all this discussion about bringing no bread? Don't you understand or grasp what I say even yet? Are your minds closed? Are you like the people who "having eyes, do not see, and having ears, do not hear"? Have you forgotten – when I broke five loaves for five thousand people, how many baskets full of pieces did you pick up?'

'Twelve,' they replied.

'And when there were seven loaves for four thousand people, how many baskets of pieces did you pick up?'

'Seven,' they said.

'And does that still mean nothing to you?' he said.

The Pharisees seem determined to secure some absolutely infallible sign from Jesus that he is indeed the Messiah. But characteristically, Jesus will have none of this. If the evidence of his teaching, his healing and his way of life do not convince them that he is what he claims to be, then he is simply not going to give them some devastating proof. The Pharisees want it both ways; they wanted to retain the attitude of aloof criticism and at the same time demanded an irrefutable demonstration of Christ's identity. This Jesus did not, and does not, ever give. It is only after a man exhibits faith in Christ and follows his way that the inward proof begins to grow. See John 7:16, 17. There are no 'detached' Christians. The sigh or deep inward groan of Jesus this time is not out of sympathy but a sign of Jesus' combined distress and exasperation at the hardened attitude of the Pharisees. It must have been very painful indeed to Jesus that his chosen disciples were so slow to grasp essential truth.

Once more aboard the boat Jesus is still concerned that his disciples should not be misled. Leaven was the form of yeast commonly used in making bread. A piece of dough from yesterday's baking might be used to start today's. The use of leaven as a simile would be quite familiar to the disciples. Its quiet, almost invisible growth, and the fact that a small quantity could permeate a large lump, made it apt enough to use as a picture of any form of influence, good or bad. Here Jesus is warning them against two bad influences, namely, the 'leaven' of the Pharisees which was the penetrating evil of narrow rigorous legality, and the 'leaven' of Herod which would be the undermining evil of worldly ambition and moral licence. The disciples, of whom it can be said politely that they were not being too bright over this matter, imagine that Jesus is referring to the fact that they are short of food. Jesus is compelled to remind them in some detail of his previous provision of food when it was necessary and makes their obtuseness almost inexcusable.

Jesus restores sight

vs 22–26 So they arrived at Bethsaida where a blind man was brought to him, with the earnest request that he should touch him. Jesus took the blind man's hand and led him outside the village. Then he moistened his eyes with saliva and putting his hands on him, asked,

'Can you see at all?'

The man looked up and said,

'I can see people. They look like trees – only they are walking about.'

Then Jesus put his hands on his eyes once more and his sight came into focus, and he recovered and saw everything sharp and clear. And Jesus sent him off to his own house with the words,

'Don't even go into the village.'

At Bethsaida Jesus performs what we might call a two-stage miracle. Once again the sufferer is brought to Jesus by his friends. At the first touch of Jesus the man's sight is partially restored; he can see people but 'they look like trees . . . walking about.' It requires a second touch from Jesus before his sight is restored to normal. This may easily be a kind of parable on Mark's part to show how the disciples came to have spiritual sight by degrees and not all at once. As in other instances of healing Jesus does not want the story spread into the village, to which in any case the man does not belong, but sends him home.

Jesus' question: Peter's inspired answer

vs 27–30 Jesus then went away with his disciples to the villages of Caesarea Philippi. On the way he asked them,

'Who are men saying that I am?'

'John the Baptist,' they answered. 'But others say that you are Elijah or, some say, one of the prophets.'

Then he asked them,

'But what about you – who do you say that I am?'

'You are Christ!' answered Peter.

Then Jesus impressed it upon them that they must not mention this to anyone.

Caesarea Philippi was so called in honour of Caesar the Emperor and Philip the tetrarch who ruled the territory.

Philip had made the capital splendid with altars, statues and votive images. Here we are concerned not with the city but with the villages nearby. It is apparently on their journey northwards that Jesus asks the disciples first what people's opinion of him is and is given the answer that in popular thought he is either John the Baptist risen from the dead, or Elijah the prophet, who was to come before the actual Messiah. Then he asks them the opinion of the disciples themselves and Peter, no doubt speaking for them all, declares that they believe that Jesus is the Christ (or Messiah).

Jesus speaks of the future and of the cost of discipleship

vs 31–38 And he began to teach them that it was inevitable that the Son of Man should go through much suffering and be utterly repudiated by the elders and chief priests and scribes, and be killed, and after three days rise again. He told them all this quite bluntly.

This made Peter draw him on one side and take him to task about what he had said. But Jesus turned and faced his disciples and rebuked Peter.

'Out of my way, Satan!' he said. 'Peter, your thoughts are not God's thoughts, but man's!'

Then he called his disciples and the people around him, and said to them,

'If anyone wants to follow in my footsteps, he must give up all right to himself, take up his cross and follow me. The man who tries to save his life will lose it; it is the man who loses his life for my sake and the gospel's who will save it. What good can it do a man to gain the whole world at the price of his own soul? What can a man offer to buy back his soul once he has lost it? If anyone is ashamed of me and my words in this unfaithful and sinful generation, the Son of Man will be ashamed of him when he comes in the Father's glory with the holy angels around him.'

No doubt to the disciples' astonishment Jesus now tells them not only that they must keep this a secret, but that he, the Son of Man, must inevitably suffer, be rejected and finally killed and rise again after three days. So bluntly does he make this prophecy that Peter rashly decides that he must intervene and say that this is no future for the Son of Man who is also God's Messiah. But Jesus turns on Peter, recognizing an old temptation, and sternly rebukes him for representing the voice of Satan and not understanding the ways of God.

Now, as much to our astonishment as to the disciples', Jesus makes some strange and, at the time, surely incomprehensible remarks to the people as well as to his chosen few. The only man who carried a cross in those days was the criminal under Roman law who was due for crucifixion, and it is difficult to see what sense this could have made at the time, even though the saying was treasured. It is an extraordinarily difficult paragraph to translate. What does Jesus mean by the expression 'deny himself' as the AV has it? The Greek word for 'life' and the Greek word for 'soul' are the same. Does Jesus mean that to give up one's ordinary natural self means gaining the real and eternal self? Certainly the whole passage sets the price of working for the Kingdom very high.

Jesus apparently demands the total surrender of selfish wishes and desires and complete loyalty to himself; by this alone can a man save his 'life' or 'soul' and no material gain can possibly compensate for the loss of the real self.

CHAPTER NINE

*

Jesus foretells his glory

vs 1–13 Then he added,

'Believe me, there are some of you standing here who will know nothing of death until you have seen the kingdom of God already come in power!'

Six days later, Jesus took Peter and James and John with him and led them high up on a hill-side where they were entirely alone. His whole appearance changed before their eyes, while his clothes became white, dazzling white – whiter than any earthly bleaching could make them. Elijah and Moses appeared to the disciples and stood there in conversation with Jesus. Peter burst out to Jesus,

'Master, it is wonderful for us to be here! Shall we put up three shelters – one for you, one for Moses and one for Elijah?'

He really did not know what to say, for they were very frightened. Then came a cloud which overshadowed them and a voice spoke out of the cloud,

'This is my dearly-loved Son. Listen to him!'

Then, quite suddenly they looked all round them and saw nobody at all with them but Jesus. And as they came down the hill-side, he warned them not to tell anybody what they had seen till 'the Son of Man should have risen again from the dead'. They were deeply impressed by this remark and tried to puzzle out among themselves what 'rising from the dead' could mean. Then they asked him this question,

'Why do the scribes say that Elijah must come before Christ?'

'It is quite true,' he told them, 'that Elijah does come first, and begins the restoration of all things. But what does the scripture say about the Son of Man? This: that he must go through much suffering and be treated with contempt! I tell you that not only has Elijah come already but they have done to him exactly what they wanted – just as the scripture says of him.'

The description of what nowadays we call the Transfiguration almost certainly came from Peter, an eye-witness. In the nature of things it is subjective. Peter describes what he saw and heard. But I would suggest that there is another way of looking at the incident: that the three chosen disciples were temporarily relieved from their earth-blindness and saw eternal reality, a dimension beyond time and space. Moses representing the Law and Elijah representing the Prophets, appear as Jesus' contemporaries and are seen to be in conversation with him. Their dazzling whiteness was a symbol of their heavenly splendour. We need, throughout the New Testament, to remember that, apart from the lightning flash, the only light that the people of those days knew was that from a feeble candle or from the wick of an oil-lamp. We, with our knowledge of light from the pocket-torch through domestic lighting, stage lighting and the vast glare of flood-lights, are familiar with the control and use of light which men of the New Testament were not. So the appearance of Jesus clothed in dazzling light would have a very strong effect upon them. Peter, naturally enough, would like to prolong this vision. The only practical way he can think of doing this is for them to put up three shelters; but of course he hardly knew what he was saying. Then came the voice from Heaven which this time is heard and understood by the disciples. The voice came from a cloud, by which the Jews often meant the very presence of God. God himself is telling Peter, James and John that this man is his Son, and what he says must be listened to.

The moments of glory do not last and once again they are in normal earthly life with only Jesus visible to them. As they come down from the hill or mountain-side Jesus warns them to say nothing about the vision until the Son of Man has risen from the dead. We can easily imagine how this must have puzzled them even though they had already been warned that the Son of Man would be persecuted, rejected, put to death and rise from that death. In all probability their minds are still filled with the idea of the Messiah being a conquering hero. Indeed, if we ourselves had not the benefit of hindsight we should find it surpassingly strange that when God himself became man he should foretell such a miserable future for himself. Although he does not say so in so many words Jesus plainly implies that 'Elijah' has already come in the person of John the Baptist, and that even the chosen messengers of God are not immune to the wickedness of men. So, he says, will it be with the Son of Man himself. The disciples are meant to realize that those who are sent by God do not enjoy special protection. Elijah suffered at the hands of Ahab and Jezebel (1 Kings 19); John the Baptist had suffered at the cruel hands of Herod, and he, Jesus, would also face contempt and suffering at the hands of men.

Jesus heals an epileptic boy

vs 14–29 Then as they rejoined the other disciples, they saw that they were surrounded by a large crowd and that some scribes were arguing with them. As soon as the people saw Jesus, they ran forward excitedly to welcome him.

'What is the trouble?' Jesus asked them.

A man from the crowd answered,

'Master, I brought my son to you because he has a dumb spirit. Wherever he is, it gets hold of him, throws him down on the ground and there he foams at the mouth and grinds his teeth. It's simply wearing him out. I did speak to your disciples to get them to drive it out, but they hadn't the power to do it.'

Jesus answered them,

'Oh, what a faithless people you are! How long must I be with you, how long must I put up with you? Bring him here to me.'

So they brought the boy to him, and as soon as the spirit saw Jesus, it convulsed the boy, who fell to the ground and writhed there, foaming at the mouth.

'How long has he been like this?' Jesus asked the father.

'Ever since he was a child,' he replied. 'Again and

again it has thrown him into the fire or into water to finish him off. But if you can do anything, please take pity on us and help us.'

'If *I* can do anything!' retorted Jesus. 'Everything is possible to the man who believes.'

'I do believe,' the boy's father burst out. 'Help me to believe more!'

When Jesus noticed that a crowd was rapidly gathering, he spoke sharply to the evil spirit, with the words,

'I command you, deaf and dumb spirit, come out of this boy, and never go into him again!'

The spirit gave a loud scream and after a dreadful convulsion left him. The boy lay there like a corpse, so that most of the bystanders said, 'He is dead.'

But Jesus grasped his hands and lifted him up, and then he stood on his own feet. When he had gone home, Jesus' disciples asked him privately,

'Why were we unable to drive it out?'

'Nothing can drive out this kind of thing except prayer,' replied Jesus.

It is sometimes said, in sermons and elsewhere, that this contrast of the splendid vision and the misery of earthly reality depicted here is typical of life. This is true enough but this particular instance is not a very good example of the contrast. For it is quite plain from Mark's terse words that the walk down the hill or mountain provided Jesus with time to explain that the sort of glory that they had witnessed was not likely to be seen in this present world; indeed the reverse was to be true, hard though it must have been for them to grasp it.

The epileptic boy whom they now meet with his father is apparently both deaf and dumb. He is the victim of frequent and violent seizures. It is indeed a harrowing picture. The blindness and faithlessness of ordinary people must have grieved and surprised Jesus. He, who lived in constant communion with his Father, could see things much more steadily and realistically. It is almost in exasperation that he says, 'how long must I be with you?' Jesus then questions the father and finds that the epilepsy has continued for some years. The father certainly shows some faith in bringing his son to Jesus but he still lacks anything like full trust. It is almost grotesque to read that he says to Jesus 'if *you* can do anything'. Jesus declares that everything is possible to the man who believes, and the father is honest enough to admit that he has faith but not enough of it. 'Help thou mine unbelief' are words that have become almost proverbial and we need to see what they really mean. Surely the man is aware that his faith is not deep enough or strong enough and he wants to believe more. Jesus commands the evil spirit, which afflicted the boy with deafness and dumbness as well as causing his epilepsy, to come out and never return. There is a final fierce convulsion of the boy's frame as the order is obeyed and the boy lies as if life had gone out of him. But Jesus takes him by his hands and sets him on his feet, alive. The disciples are naturally surprised that, although they had been given the power to drive out evil spirits, this particular case had been too much for them. Jesus' reply is mystifying. We can discount the 'fasting' which was an early addition and does not appear in the best manuscripts. But does Jesus mean that his disciples had not used the power of prayer enough, or that they had not by prayer increased their own faith enough? He himself, as we know, took periods off for solitary prayer to renew his communion with his Father. Perhaps we Christians of today forget the necessity of constant prayer if we are to be effective against the powers of evil however they are shown.

Jesus privately warns his disciples of his own death

vs 30–32 Then they left that district and went straight through Galilee. Jesus kept this journey secret for he was teaching his disciples that the Son of Man would be betrayed into the power of men, that they would kill him and that three days after his death he would rise again. But they were completely mystified by this saying, and were afraid to question him about it.

Presumably Jesus kept his journey secret by avoiding the high-roads and thus keeping free from the crowds and enabling him to teach his disciples further. Once again he tells them how the Son of Man will be betrayed and killed and after three days rise again. At this stage they are completely mystified as to what he could possibly mean. Yet he plainly speaks with such force and authority that they did not dare to question him about it.

Jesus defines the new 'greatness'

vs 33–42 So they came to Capernaum. And when they were indoors he asked them,

'What were you discussing as we came along the road?'

They were silent, for on the way they had been arguing about who should be the greatest. Jesus sat down and called the twelve, and said to them,

'If any man wants to be first, he must be last and servant of all.'

Then he took a little child and stood him in front of them all, and putting his arm round him, said to them,

'Anyone who welcomes one little child like this for my sake is welcoming me. And the man who welcomes me is welcoming not only me but the one who sent me!'

Then John said to him,

'Master, we saw somebody driving out evil spirits in your name, and we tried to stop him, for he is not one who follows us.'

But Jesus replied,

'You must not stop him. No one who exerts such

power in my name would readily say anything against me. For the man who is not against us is on our side. In fact, I assure you that the man who gives you a mere drink of water in my name, because you are followers of mine, will most certainly be rewarded. And I tell you too, that the man who disturbs the faith of one of the humblest of those who believe in me would be better off if he were thrown into the sea with a great mill-stone hung round his neck!'

Jesus probably has a good idea of what the disciples had been talking about on the way to Capernaum. Quite possibly he had overheard brief snatches of their conversation. Anyway, he is determined that they shall learn the difference between grandness and greatness. In this new kingdom greatness is to be found not in rank or position but in the willingness to serve humbly.

The little child was presumably playing nearby or had wandered in from a nearby room, since they were indoors. Jesus takes him with simple affection. It is the humility and openness of the little child which Jesus is commending. He is also saying that anyone who recognizes this childlike spirit is recognizing Christ himself, and not only Christ but God who sent him.

John is rarely the spokesman in the Gospels. Here (v. 38), probably speaking for them all, he says that they have tried to stop someone from driving out evil spirits in Jesus' name. That, it must have seemed, was the special power Jesus had given to them. But Jesus realizes that no harm could come from leaving such a case alone. A man who was as yet outside his company, but was acting in accordance with his will, could not be regarded as an enemy. Not only actions of power like this, but the act of a simple piece of service like giving a drink to the disciples because they belonged to Christ would not pass unnoticed. The opposite is terribly true. Those who think of Jesus as meek and mild would do well to ponder on these words. Jesus says in effect that a man would be better off dead than to cause a spiritual injury to one of his humblest followers. In today's muddled theology the principle of special care for the weak in faith seems to have been forgotten. But it is obviously very important to Jesus and he carries it into men's private lives. Of course the words are meant to be taken metaphorically but none the less seriously.

Entering the kingdom may mean painful sacrifice

vs 43–50 'Indeed, if it is your own hand that spoils your faith, you must cut it off. It is better for you to enter life maimed than to keep both your hands and go to the rubbish-heap, where the fire never dies. If your foot spoils your faith, you must cut it off. It is better for you to enter life on one foot than to keep both your feet and be thrown on to the rubbish-heap. And if your eye leads you astray, pluck it out. It is better for you to go one-eyed into the kingdom of God than to keep both eyes and be thrown on to the rubbish-heap, where decay never stops and the fire never goes out. For everyone will be salted with fire. Salt is a good thing; but if it should lose its saltiness, what can you do to restore its flavour? You must have salt in yourselves, and live at peace with each other.'

There may be parts of a man's personality which need to be severely controlled or even denied entirely if there is a possibility of that part of him making the whole man only fit for the rubbish-dump. The idea of the unquenchable fire is derived from the name Gehenna, a ravine where refuse and rubbish of all kinds from the city of Jerusalem perpetually burned. It may well be that we have not got the complete text here, for the connection between the fires of Gehenna and every sacrifice being salted with fire is far from clear. It is very difficult to know what Jesus meant. Possibly it, rather

obscurely, means that every Christian life will be touched with
the fire of persecution and so 'salted'. There may also be
some connection with the Levitical regulation that salt was to
be added to all offerings (Leviticus 2:13). Its general meaning
seems to be that by self-sacrifice and vigilance the Christian
life is continually saved from insipidity. His disciples are to
maintain the habit of self-denial and humility and thus live at
peace with each other.

CHAPTER TEN

*

The divine purpose in marriage

vs 1–12 Then he got up and left Galilee and went off
to the borders of Judea and beyond the Jordan. Again
great crowds assembled to meet him, and again, according to his custom, he taught them. Then some Pharisees
arrived to ask him this test-question,

'Is it right for a man to divorce his wife?'

Jesus replied by asking them,

'What has Moses commanded you to do?'

'Moses allows men to write a divorce-notice and then
to dismiss her,' they said.

'Moses gave you that commandment,' returned Jesus,
'because you know so little of the meaning of love. But
from the beginning of the creation, God made them male
and female. "For this cause shall a man leave his father
and mother, and shall cleave to his wife; and the twain
shall become one flesh." So that in body they are no
longer two people but one. That is why man must never
separate what God has joined together.'

On reaching the house, his disciples questioned him
again about this matter.

'Any man who divorces his wife and marries another

woman,' he told them, 'commits adultery against his wife. And if she herself divorces her husband and marries someone else, she commits adultery.'

In asking this question about divorce the Pharisees are plainly trying to get Jesus to contradict Moses (see Deuteronomy 24:1–4). In his reply Jesus indicates that it is only because of 'the hardness of men's hearts' or, as I have translated it because men 'know so little of the meaning of love', that Moses made this concession. Divorce is no part of the divine plan, which implies that a man and a woman should become so close that they could be regarded as one person. Jesus repeats this uncompromising attitude to his disciples later when they are indoors. We may perhaps argue today that in certain cases there never was a true marriage, but the divine principle remains clear.

He welcomes small children

vs 13–16 Then some people came to him bringing little children for him to touch. The disciples tried to discourage them. When Jesus saw this, he was indignant and told them,

'You must let little children come to me – never stop them! For the kingdom of God belongs to such as these. Indeed, I assure you that the man who does not accept the kingdom of God like a little child will never enter it.'

Then he took the children in his arms and laid his hands on them and blessed them.

We may wonder why the disciples should discourage people from bringing the children for Jesus to touch them. Perhaps they thought it was unbecoming to his dignity or a mere distraction from his work. But it is obvious that children are precious to Jesus. Not only are they to be valued for their own sake but their unspoiled qualities of simplicity, trustfulness and willingness to learn are the very qualities which a man must have if he is to enter the Kingdom. Jesus endorses his words by laying his hands on the children and blessing them.

Jesus shows the danger of riches

vs 17–31 As he began to take the road again, a man came running up and fell at his feet and asked him,

'Good Master, tell me, please, what must I do to be sure of eternal life?'

'Why do you call me good?' returned Jesus. 'No one is good – only God. You know the commandments, "Do no murder, Do not commit adultery, Do not steal, Do not bear false witness, Do not cheat, Honour thy father and mother." '

'Master,' he replied, 'I have carefully kept all these since I was quite young.'

Jesus looked steadily at him, and his heart warmed towards him. Then he said,

'There is one thing you still need. Go and sell everything you have, give the money away to the poor – you will have riches in Heaven. And then come back and follow me.'

At these words his face fell and he went away in deep distress, for he was very rich. Then Jesus looked round at them all, and said to his disciples,

'How difficult it is for those who have great possessions to enter the kingdom of God !'

The disciples were staggered at these words, but Jesus continued,

'Children, you don't know how hard it is to get into the kingdom of God. Why, a camel could more easily pass through the eye of a needle than a rich man get into the kingdom of God.'

At this their astonishment knew no bounds, and they said to each other,

'Then who can possibly be saved?'

Jesus looked straight at them and said,

'Humanly speaking it is impossible, but not with God. Everything is possible with God.'

Then Peter burst out,

'But look, we have left everything and followed you!'

'I promise you,' returned Jesus, 'that nobody has left home or brothers or sisters or mother or father or children or land for my sake and the gospel's without getting back a hundred times over, now in this present life, homes and brothers and sisters, mothers and children and land – though not without persecution – and in the next world eternal life. But many who are first now will then be last, and the last now will then be first.'

Matthew tells us that this eager man who sought out Jesus was young. Mark merely indicates his eagerness and humility. Jesus' reply is at first sight rather puzzling. It is not in fact that he is denying that he is himself good, but that he wants to direct the young man's attention to God to whom his first loyalty must be given. He has the insight to detect the young man's real trouble. He wants to secure 'eternal life' by keeping the commandments he knows and any others that Jesus may impose upon him. But Jesus can see what he needs is to commit himself to *being*, not to mere external *doing*. In his case, to become a follower of Jesus, he must throw away the luxuries and cushioning that the possession of riches provides. He must be stripped to his bare self and then come and follow Jesus.

We know nothing of the subsequent history of this rich young man but for the moment he goes away crestfallen. Jesus gives one of his searching looks at the surrounding faces and tells men how difficult it is for those with great possessions to enter the Kingdom. Later, presumably, he repeats this truth to his close disciples. It staggers them because to many

Jews of that time material prosperity was regarded as a sign of God's blessing. They feel that if those who have been signally blessed by this world's goods will find it almost impossible to enter the Kingdom, how much more difficult will it be for those who have little material blessing. This elicits an enigmatic reply from Jesus, 'Everything is possible with God.'

It would seem as we look down the centuries at the lives of fully committed Christians that some have indeed been required to give up all their worldly goods; others have been required to make considerable sacrifices; others again have been required to live with their riches and dispose of them wisely and usefully. It would be foolish to argue from this single incident that every true follower of Jesus must give away his every possession. Peter, with characteristic forthrightness, immediately points out that they, the Apostles, have at least done what the rich young man did not. They have given up their work, their homes and their friends in order to follow him; what would be *their* reward? Jesus replies that in the life of the Kingdom any sacrifice is more than repaid, 'now in this present life', It will be found that God is no man's debtor, and that a man will be more than recompensed by a wide circle of friends and homes and indeed all that he has sacrificed, in this present life. This is a saying that many a missionary in our present age has found to be true. But Jesus adds the words 'though not without persecution' and at the end of this temporary life the man who is fully committed will enter upon the timeless life of God. He further adds that this world's values will often be reversed by the values of the Kingdom; those who are rich and powerful will be found to be poor and weak under the new way of looking at things. Similarly many a humble and apparently unimportant person may be valued highly under the conditions of the kingdom of God.

The last journey to Jerusalem begins

vs 32–34 They were now on their way going up to Jerusalem and Jesus walked on ahead. The disciples were dismayed at this, and those who followed were afraid. Then once more he took the twelve aside and began to tell them what was going to happen to him.

'We are now going up to Jerusalem,' he said, 'as you can see. And the Son of Man will be betrayed into the power of the chief priests and scribes. They are going to condemn him to death and hand him over to pagans who will jeer at him and spit at him and flog him and kill him. But after three days he will rise again.'

Jesus now strides ahead as though set to meet the doom he foresees for himself, and his followers are afraid to keep up with him. Then he pauses and makes one more attempt to explain to the Twelve what is going to happen – how disgrace, degradation and final death will come to him, the Son of Man, but that he will rise again. That he said these things was probably remembered by Peter recalling them for Mark to set down.

An ill-timed request

vs 35–45 Then Zebedee's two sons James and John approached him, saying,

'Master, we want you to do for us whatever we ask.'

'What do you want me to do for you?' answered Jesus.

'Give us permission to sit one on each side of you when you reign in your glory!'

'You don't know what you are asking,' Jesus said to them. 'Can you drink the cup I have to drink? Can you go through the baptism I have to bear?'

'Yes, we can,' they replied.

Then Jesus told them,

'You will indeed drink the cup I am drinking, and you will undergo the baptism which I have to bear! But as for sitting on either side of me, that is not for me to give – such places belong to those for whom they are prepared.'

When the other ten heard about this, they began to be highly indignant with James and John; so Jesus called them all to him, and said,

'You know that the so-called rulers of the heathen lord it over them, and their great men have absolute power. But it must not be so among you. No, whoever among you wants to be great must become the servant of you all, and if he wants to be first among you he must be the slave of all men! For the Son of Man himself has not come to be served but to serve, and to give his life to set many others free.'

That they were still unable to understand what he was talking about is shown by the ill-timed request of James and John. Jesus directly challenges these two and asks them whether they are able to drink the cup that he is going to drink and suffer the 'baptism' that he is going to bear. Both these metaphors for suffering and distress would be familiar to them from the Old Testament. 'The cup of suffering' occurs several times in the Psalms and someone who is in dire affliction is also considered by the Psalmists to have 'passed through deep waters'. For baptism does not really mean a casual sprinkling but a deep immersion in water. Jesus tells them that they will indeed experience the kind of suffering he is going to bear, but he cannot promise them seats on either side of him in his kingdom. Such positions of honour are already reserved for those for whom they have been prepared. See Matthew 20:23. The other ten are highly indignant with James and John, probably not because their request is so ill-timed in the circumstances but because it seems to be a piece of sheer selfishness. Once again Jesus has to tell them that the rules in the Kingdom are quite different from those in the pagan world. It is not the man who flaunts his power but the man who embraces a thorough-going humility who is to be great.

'It must not be so among you.' We may sometimes wonder how seriously the Church as a whole has taken this teaching. It would not be difficult to show that there are degrees and positions in the Christian Church which seem very like those of the surrounding pagan world. But this is plainly not Jesus' intention. It is the man who serves who will be considered great and the Son of Man himself 'has not come to be served but to serve, and to give his life to set many others free'. Literally this last saying means to give his life as 'a ransom in place of many', and much theological ink has been spilt in discussing to whom such a ransom has to be paid. Certainly it is not a ransom to be paid to the Devil as many mediaevalists believed. And we cannot imagine God the Father demanding a ransom payment as the price for setting his children free. But in all serious religions there is always the problem of reconciliation between the holiness of God and the sinfulness of man. Probably Paul comes as near as anyone to the truth when he writes, 'God was in Christ reconciling the world unto himself' (2 Corinthians 5:19).

Jesus heals a blind beggar

*vs 46–52 Then they came to Jericho, and as he was leaving it accompanied by his disciples and a large crowd, Bartimaeus (that is, the son of Timaeus), a blind beggar, was sitting by the side of the road. When he heard that it was Jesus of Nazareth he began to call out,

'Jesus, Son of David, have pity on me!'

Many of the people told him sharply to keep quiet, but he shouted all the more,

'Son of David, have pity on me!'

* It is perfectly possible that this passage is misplaced.

Jesus stood quite still and said,
'Call him here.'
So they called the blind man, saying,
'It's all right now, get up, he's calling you!'
At this he threw off his coat, jumped to his feet and
came to Jesus.
'What do you want me to do for you?' he asked him.
The blind man answered,
'Oh, Master, let me see again!'
'Go on your way then,' returned Jesus, 'your faith has
healed you.'
And he recovered his sight at once and followed Jesus
along the road.

We have no idea why Jesus came to Jericho or why he was
now leaving it. The healing of the blind beggar is put by Luke
as if it were done as he approached the city, but as this is
likely to be the recollection of Peter, Mark's version is to be
preferred. Somehow or other this blind beggar hears that
Jesus is passing his way and he calls out to him for mercy,
using the Messianic title, 'Son of David'. Jesus calls him and
the blind man, jumping to his feet, throws off his outer gar-
ment and comes to Jesus. Again this little touch suggests a
detail noticed by an eye-witness. He uses the word 'Rabboni'
which is the Aramaic for 'Master' or 'Lord' and we may
compare this with Mary's sudden recognition of her risen
Lord (John 20:16). Jesus heals the man, making it quite clear
that it is his faith that has healed him, and this time the
healed man is allowed to follow Jesus along the road.

CHAPTER ELEVEN

*

Jesus arranges for his entry into the city

vs 1–19 When they were approaching Jerusalem and had come to Bethphage and Bethany near the Mount of Olives, he sent off two of his disciples with these instructions,

'Go into the village just ahead of you and as soon as you enter it you will find a tethered colt on which no one has yet ridden. Untie it, and bring it here. If anybody asks you, "Why are you doing this?", just say, "His master needs him, and will send him back immediately." '

So they went off and found the colt tethered by a doorway outside in the open street, and they untied it. Some of the bystanders did say, 'What are you doing, untying this colt?', but they made the reply Jesus told them to make, and the men raised no objection. So they brought the colt to Jesus, threw their coats on its back, and he took his seat upon it.

Many of the people spread out their coats in his path as he rode along, and others put down rushes which they had cut from the fields. The whole crowd, both those who were in front and those who were behind Jesus, shouted,

'God save him! – God bless the one who comes in the name of the Lord! God bless the coming kingdom of our father David! God save him from on high!'

Jesus entered Jerusalem and went into the Temple and looked round on all that was going on. And then, since it was already late in the day, he went out to Bethany with the twelve.

On the following day, when they had left Bethany, Jesus felt hungry. He noticed a fig-tree in the distance covered with leaves, and he walked up to it to see if he could find any fruit on it. But when he got to it, he could find nothing but leaves, for it was not yet the season for figs. Then Jesus spoke to the tree,

'May nobody ever eat fruit from you !'

And the disciples heard him say it.

Then they came into Jerusalem and Jesus went into the Temple and began to drive out those who were buying and selling there. He over-turned the tables of the money-changers and the benches of the dove-sellers, and he would not allow anyone to make a short cut through the Temple when carrying such things as water-pots. And he began to teach them and said,

'Doesn't the scripture say, "My house shall be called a house of prayer for all nations"? But you have turned it into a thieves' kitchen !'

The chief priests and scribes heard him say this and tried to find a way of getting rid of him. But they were in fact afraid of him, for his teaching had captured the imagination of the people. And every evening they left the city.

We cannot identify Bethphage but Bethany was a village lying rather less than two miles from Jericho on the slopes of the Mount of Olives. We remember that it was in this village that Simon the leper had his home and so did Martha, Mary and Lazarus. It appears to have been used by Jesus as a resting-place in between his visits to Jerusalem.

It now looks as though we enter upon a scheme prearranged by Jesus. There is no need to see anything miraculous in Jesus' knowing that the colt would be where he said it would be or that its owner would allow it to be borrowed. It would be pretty certain that it was an ass's colt, not only because Jesus was fulfilling the prophecy of Zechariah 9:9,

but because the use of an ass as a mount signified peace
rather than the horse, which signified war. As the Passover
approached, the hope of the Jews of their Messiah arriving
in power to set them free from the hated Roman yoke would
be rising to fever-heat. Jesus is in effect saying, 'Yes, your
Messiah has come but he comes in peace and not in war.'

Nevertheless it was accepted as a triumphal progress, for
people at the height of their emotion spread their coats in his
path, or even rushes and brushwood cut from the fields nearby. Hosanna literally means, 'O save' and is a little difficult
to translate into meaningful English.

The real Messiah is not leading them in revolt and he goes
not to the Roman garrison but to the Jews' own Temple.
This would have been into the outer courts of the Temple
where the buying, selling, money-changing and other abuses
were going on. Apparently after looking round on all this
Jesus did nothing for the moment but retired to Bethany with
the Twelve.

On the next day we find this extraordinary incident of the
cursing of the fig-tree. The fig-tree in question was in full leaf
and so should have had upon it some fruit, if not yet ripe.
Possibly to Jesus it was a symbol of the nation to whom he
belonged and whom he had come to save. It showed all the
outward signs of a flourishing religion but was in fact barren.
It could be that Jesus' terrible sense of frustration and
righteous anger exploded in this attack upon the pretentious
but worthless fig-tree. We are very apt to forget the tension
under which Jesus was living, and how bitterly his hopes for
his people had been disappointed. Mark alone records that
the disciples heard Jesus venting his feeling of frustration and
despair upon the fig-tree.

Now Jesus goes into action. The very part of the Temple
which should have been a place of 'prayer for all nations'
(Isaiah 56:7) had become no more than a market-place with
a fair amount of sharp dealing going on. The place which
had been meant to be a place of prayer and worship was, for

the sake of pure convenience, used for money-changing (for the Temple tax had to be paid in Jewish money), the sale of sacrificial animals, especially doves, and as a short cut for carrying water-pots and other household articles. This had happened because the Jews had become blind to the original purpose of the outer court of the Temple and had, through sheer greed and sloth, allowed it to become 'a thieves' kitchen'. This is one of the few occasions when the wrath of Jesus is recorded and he sets about clearing the Temple court in no uncertain way. Naturally the chief priests and scribes heard of this violence but, though they longed to destroy him, could do nothing as yet. For the great mass of people who had heard his teaching had had their imagination caught by this young reformer who was plainly speaking the truth of God. Apparently unmolested, Jesus retires to Bethany each evening after teaching in the Temple.

Jesus talks of faith, prayer and forgiveness

vs 20–25 One morning as they were walking along, they noticed that the fig-tree had withered away from the roots. Peter remembered it, and said,

'Master, look, the fig-tree that you cursed is all shrivelled up !'

'Have faith in God,' replied Jesus to them. 'I tell you that if anyone should say to this hill, "Get up and throw yourself into the sea", and without any doubt in his heart believe that what he says will happen, then it *will* happen ! That is why I tell you, whatever you pray about and ask for, believe that you have received it and it will be yours. And whenever you stand praying, you must forgive any grudge that you are holding against anyone else, and your Heavenly Father will forgive you *your* sins.'

The fig-tree, which was probably planted by the road-side,

has now withered away, and Peter calls Jesus' attention to the result of his previous curse. The reply of Jesus may seem to have little relevance but I venture, as an opinion only, to say that Jesus is underlining the enormous power of faith in God. The man who lives in faithful dependence on God can not only destroy a worthless fig-tree but can cast mountains into the sea. (This was a favourite figure of speech in Jesus' day. Rabbis of unusual spiritual influence were described as 'removers of mountains'.) Prayer with faith has no limit to its power. But such prayer must be made without bitterness in the heart against anyone. No one can be truly in touch with God his Father unless he is living in love and charity with his fellow-men.

Jesus' authority is directly challenged

vs 27–33 So they came once more to Jerusalem, and while Jesus was walking in the Temple, the chief priests, scribes and elders approached him, and asked,

'What authority have you for what you're doing? And who gave you permission to do these things?'

'I am going to ask you a question,' replied Jesus, 'and if you answer me, I will tell you what authority I have for what I do. The baptism of John, now – did it come from Heaven or was it purely human? Tell me that.'

At this they argued with each other, 'If we say from Heaven, he will say, "then why didn't you believe in him?" but if we say it was purely human, well . . .' For they were frightened of the people, since all of them believed that John was a real prophet. So they answered Jesus,

'We do not know.'

'Then I cannot tell you by what authority I do these things,' returned Jesus.

Jesus evidently paid several visits to Jerusalem at the Passover time. This time he is questioned by the priests, the scribes and the elders together. Very naturally having seen or heard of what he has done in the Temple court they demand to know his authority for acting as he has. In characteristic fashion Jesus answers one question with another. This is not merely a form of verbal fencing but it makes the original questioner find the answer to his question in his own heart. So Jesus asks them about the baptism of John. They are caught between the fact that they did not believe in him as a prophet and that they are now too frightened to say so because the popular feeling is certainly that he was. Thus they cannot give an answer nor do they deserve one.

CHAPTER TWELVE

*

Jesus tells a story, with a pointed application

vs 1–12 Then he began to talk to them in parables.

'A man once planted a vineyard,' he said, 'fenced it round, dug out the hole for the wine-press and built a watch-tower. Then he let it out to some farm-workers and went abroad. At the end of the season he sent a servant to the tenants to receive his share of the vintage. But they got hold of him, knocked him about and sent him off empty-handed. The owner tried again. He sent another servant to them, but this one they knocked on the head and generally insulted. Once again he sent them another servant, but him they murdered. He sent many others and some they beat up and some they murdered. He had one man left – his own son who was very dear to him. He sent him last of all to the tenants, saying to himself, "They will surely respect my own son." But they said to each other, "This fellow is the future owner – come on, let's kill him, and the property will be ours!" So they got hold of him and murdered him, and threw his body out of the vineyard. What do you suppose the owner of the vineyard is going to do? He will come and destroy the men who were working his vineyard and will hand it over to others. Have you never read this scripture –

The stone which the builders rejected,
The same was made the head of the corner;
This was from the Lord,
And it is marvellous in our eyes?'

At this they longed to get their hands on him, for they knew perfectly well that he had aimed this parable at them – but they were afraid of the people. So they left him and went away.

This is a very obvious parable. God has done all that he can to prepare his vineyard, providing it with a fence, a watch-tower and a wine-press. He sends servants, or slaves, to collect the harvest when it is due, but they are maltreated or murdered. Finally the owner decides to send his son, expecting that at least they will treat him properly and hand over the fruits of the vineyard. But they murdered him also, hoping to get the product of the vineyard for themselves. Is it not natural, then, that the owner of the vineyard will come and destroy the tenants and hand over the vineyard to others who can be relied upon to work it honestly? This is a perfectly transparent parable of what God has done in trying to build up his vineyard, i.e. his chosen people, and they have behaved disgracefully and are even prepared to kill his own Son. The 'stone' would be understood by the Jews to be the foundation-stone. Jesus is, in effect, telling the Jewish leaders exactly how through the centuries they have abused and killed the prophets whom God sent to them, and even now are preparing to murder his own Son. Yet the 'stone' which they are rejecting will become the foundation-stone of God's building. Again it is only their fear of the people which saves Jesus from their violence.

> Six days later, Jesus took Peter and James and John with him and led them high up on a hill-side where they were entirely alone. (Mark 9:2)

A test question

vs 13–17 Later they sent some of the Pharisees and some of the Herod-party to trap him in an argument. They came up and said to him,

'Master, we know that you are an honest man and that you are not swayed by men's opinion of you. Obviously you don't care for human approval but teach the way of God with the strictest regard for truth – is it right to pay tribute to Caesar or not : are we to pay or not to pay?'

But Jesus saw through their hypocrisy and said to them,

'Why try this trick on me? Bring me a coin and let me look at it.'

So they brought one to him.

'Whose face is this?' asked Jesus, 'and whose name is in the inscription?'

'Caesar's,' they replied. And Jesus said,

'Then pay to Caesar what belongs to Caesar, and to God what belongs to God!' – a reply which staggered them.

Once more we get this strange alliance of the Herodians and the Pharisees joining in their enmity to Jesus. The Roman tax had to be paid in Roman coin, and naturally Jesus' enemies are hoping that he will say that it is wrong to pay a tax to a Gentile power. But he asks to see a coin stamped with the effigy of the Roman emperor's head, in this case that of Tiberius. Jesus sees nothing wrong in paying that for which the civil authority provides, but he reminds them of something of far greater importance: that they are to give themselves to God, for they are men who are stamped with the image of God. Such a reply naturally 'staggered them', for they were expecting a controversial answer which might be used against him.

Then they sang a hymn and went out [from Jerusalem] to the Mount of Olives. (Mark 14:26)

Jesus reveals the ignorance of the Sadducees

vs 18–27 Then some of the Sadducees (a party which maintains that there is no resurrection) approached him, and put this question to him,

'Master, Moses instructed us that if a man's brother dies leaving a widow but no child, then the man should marry the woman and raise children for his brother. Now there were seven brothers, and the first one married and died without leaving issue. Then the second one married the widow and died leaving no issue behind him. The same thing happened with the third, and indeed the whole seven died without leaving any child behind them. Finally the woman herself died. Now in this "resurrection", when men rise up again, whose wife is she going to be – for she was the wife of all seven of them?'

Jesus replied, 'Does not this show where you go wrong – and how you fail to understand both the scriptures and the power of God? When people rise from the dead they neither marry nor are they given in marriage; they live like the angels in Heaven. But as for this matter of the dead being raised, have you never read in the book of Moses, in the passage about the bush, how God spoke to him in these words, "I am the God of Abraham and the God of Isaac and the God of Jacob"? God is not God of the dead but of living men! That is where you make your great mistake.'

It is ironical that the Sadducees, who did not believe in any resurrection, should put a further trick question to him. If there is no life after death then the sort of situation which they imagine could never arise.

Jesus answers them on their own ground. They prided themselves on their knowledge of the Scriptures and consequently on the nature and methods of God. First Jesus assures them that after what is commonly called death, life is of an entirely different quality; men 'live iike the angels in Heaven'. But the second and more important mistake that they make is to think of God as the God of the past. In the incident of the burning bush God says to Moses 'I *am*' not 'I *was*' the God of Abraham and the God of Isaac and the God of Jacob. In God's real world there is no past, only an eternal present, and the Sadducees with their scrupulous study of the Scriptures ought to have known this.

The most important commandments

vs 28–34 Then one of the scribes approached him. He had been listening to the discussion, and had noticed how well Jesus had answered them, and he put this question to him,

'What are we to consider the greatest commandment of all?'

'The first and most important one is this,' Jesus replied – ' "Hear, O Israel: The Lord our God, the Lord is one: and thou shalt love the Lord thy God with all thy heart, and with all thy soul, and with all thy mind, and with all thy strength." The second is this, "Thou shalt love thy neighbour as thyself." No other commandment is greater than these.'

'I am well answered, master,' replied the scribe. 'You are absolutely right when you say that there is one God and no other God exists but him; and to love him with the whole of our hearts, the whole of our intelligence and the whole of our strength, and to love our neighbours as ourselves is infinitely more important than all these burnt-offerings and sacrifices.'

Then Jesus, noting the wisdom of his reply, said to him,

'You are not far from the kingdom of God!'

After this nobody felt they could ask him any more questions.

The scribe who now approaches Jesus comes very close to the truth of real religion. He can see that complete love of God and love of our neighbours as ourselves is far more important than any number of burnt-offerings and sacrifices. He is beginning to come near to the heart of the matter and Jesus tells him that he is not far from the kingdom of God. We can imagine that this discarding of all that was unnecessary, and which could in fact be a substitute for real worship, astonished Jesus' hearers who were, in their ordinary lives, bound up with an infinite number of rules and regulations. He has given them such an astonishing answer that for the moment they have no more questions to ask.

Jesus criticizes the scribes' teaching and behaviour

vs 35–44 Later, while Jesus was teaching in the Temple, he remarked,

'How can the scribes maintain that Christ is David's *son*, for David himself, inspired by the Holy Spirit, said,

The Lord said unto my *Lord*,

Sit thou on my right hand,

Till I make thine enemies the footstool of thy feet.

David is himself calling Christ 'Lord' – where do they get the idea that he is his son?'

The vast crowd heard this with great delight, and Jesus continued in his teaching.

'Be on your guard against these scribes who love to walk about in long robes and to be greeted respectfully in public and to have the front seats in the synagogue and the best places at dinner-parties! These are the men who grow fat on widows' property and cover up what they are doing by making lengthy prayers. They are only adding to the severity of their punishment!'

Then Jesus sat down opposite the Temple almsbox and watched the people putting their money into it. A great many rich people put in large sums. Then a poor widow came up and dropped in two little coins, worth together about a farthing. Jesus called his disciples to his side and said to them,

'Believe me, this poor widow has put in more than all the others. For they have all put in what they can easily afford, but she in her poverty who needs so much, has given away everything, her whole living!'

Jesus is now able to resume his teaching which has been interrupted by questions and he asks one of his own which the scribes find it impossible to answer. It was universally supposed that the Messiah was to be of the line of David. How then, asks Jesus, can David, inspired by the Holy Spirit, say in Psalm 110:1 that his descendant is to be his 'Lord'? The scribes and Pharisees were not prepared to admit that the Messiah would be a human being, but thought that he would be in some sense superhuman. Yet they equally emphatically taught that he was to be a descendant of David. Jesus is, in effect, saying that David's descendant is there before them but they will not recognize him, yet the well-accepted fact was that David, prophesying of the Messiah, speaks of him both as his descendant and his Lord. The crowd heard this gladly partly because of the inimical attitude of the scribes towards Jesus and partly because Jesus is assuring them that the Messiah is a normal human being.

Jesus now warns them about the scribes' ostentation, ambition and greed. By the Law the scribes administered the property of widows, but Jesus is directly accusing them of lining their own pockets at the same time. Their hypocrisy in covering up such actions is not really in the least mitigated by their 'lengthy prayers'; indeed this hypocrisy makes them the more guilty.

The 'almsbox' was really a series of trumpet-like receptacles into which gifts large or small could be placed. Many people gave large sums to the Temple, and no doubt thought themselves the better for it. But the poor widow does not escape

Jesus' eye, and he declares roundly that she, who has apparently given so little, has in fact given more than all the rest. Jesus appears to be contrasting the giving away of her whole livelihood by a poor woman with the ostentatious giving of the rich.

CHAPTER THIRTEEN

*

Jesus prophesies the ruin of the Temple

vs 1–11 Then as Jesus was leaving the Temple, one of his disciples said to him,

'Look, Master, what wonderful stonework, what a size these buildings are!'

Jesus replied,

'You see these great buildings? Not a single stone will be left standing on another; every one will be thrown down!'

Then, while he was sitting on the slope of the Mount of Olives facing the Temple, Peter, James, John and Andrew asked him privately,

'Tell us, when will these things happen? What sign will there be that all these things are going to come to an end?'

So Jesus began to tell them:

'Be very careful that no one deceives you. Many are going to come in my name and say, "I am he", and will lead many astray. When you hear of wars and rumours of wars, don't be alarmed. Such things are bound to happen, but the end is not yet. Nation will take up arms against nation and kingdom against kingdom. There will be earthquakes in different places and famines too. But these are only the beginning of birth-pangs. You yourselves must keep your wits about you, for men will hand

you over to their councils, and will beat you in their
synagogues. You will have to stand in front of rulers and
kings for my sake to bear your witness to them. For
before the end comes the gospel must be proclaimed to
all nations. But when they are taking you off to trial, do
not worry beforehand about what you are going to say
– simply say the words you are given when the time
comes. For it is not really you who will speak, but the
Holy Spirit.'

The Herodian Temple was certainly a magnificent building,
although we do not know why the disciples should have
chosen this moment to point out its splendour to Jesus. But
Jesus is not impressed. Whether it was by prophetic insight
or simply that he knew that his own rejection by the leaders
of the Jews would lead to disaster, and that it was not this
kind of magnificence that he was looking for, we don't know.
Certainly his words came true and in some forty years
Jerusalem was little more than a heap of stones.

The original four disciples of the Twelve now ask Jesus
when such terrible things will happen, and what sign there will
be of the beginning of the disasters. In his reply Jesus speaks
in the style of the prophets. He can see catastrophes, persecutions, miseries and death, but like the prophets he speaks
with no time-scale.

Jesus foretells utter misery

vs 12–20 'A brother is going to betray his own brother
to death, and a father his own child. Children will stand
up against their parents and condemn them to death.
There will come a time when the whole world will hate
you because you are known as my followers. Yet the man
who holds out to the end will be saved.

'But when you see "the abomination of desolation"
standing where it ought not – (let the reader take note

of this) – then those who are in Judea must take to the hills! The man on his house-top must not go down nor go into his house to fetch anything out of it, and the man in the field must not turn back to fetch his coat. Alas for the women who are pregnant at that time, and alas for those with babies at their breasts! Pray that it may not be winter when that time comes, for there will be such utter misery in those days as has never been from God's creation until now – and never will be again. Indeed, if the Lord did not shorten those days, no human being would survive. But for the sake of the people whom he has chosen he has shortened those days.'

Certainly wars and rumours of wars did increase until the time of the destruction of the Temple in AD 70. Equally certainly many false leaders arose. There were going to be terrible persecutions and betrayals between members of the same family. The 'abomination of desolation' may have been the placing of the Roman standards and eagles in the holy place of the Temple, or it may refer to the outrages of the conqueror Antiochus Epiphanes, who placed a heathen altar upon the Jewish altar of burnt-offering. Some particular and revolting desecration of the Jewish Temple is implied by the words 'let the reader take note of this.' These few words were inserted by Mark himself or some subsequent editor.

He warns against false christs, and commands vigilance

vs 21–37   'If anyone tells you at that time, "Look, here is Christ", or "Look, there he is", don't believe it! For false christs and false prophets will arise and will perform signs and wonders, to deceive, if it be possible, even the men of God's choice. You must keep your eyes open! I am giving you this warning before all these things happen.

'But, in those days, when that misery is past, the light

of the sun will be darkened and the moon will not give her light; stars will be falling from the sky and the powers of the heaven will rock on their foundations. Then men shall see the Son of Man coming in the clouds with great power and glory. And then shall he send out the angels to gather his chosen together from every quarter, from furthest earth to highest heaven. Let the fig-tree illustrate this for you : when its branches grow tender and produce leaves, you know that summer is near. So when you see these things happening, you may know that he is near, at your very doors! I tell you that this generation will not have passed until all these things have come true. Earth and sky will pass away, but what I have told you will never pass away! But no one knows the day or the hour of this happening, not even the angels in Heaven, no, not even the Son – only the Father. Keep your eyes open, keep on the alert, for you do not know when the time will be. It is as if a man who is travelling abroad had left his house and handed it over to be managed by his servants. He has given each one his work to do and has ordered the doorkeeper to be on the look-out. Just so must you keep a look-out, for you do not know when the master of the house will come – it might be late evening, or midnight, or cock-crow, or early morning – otherwise he might come unexpectedly and find you sound asleep. What I am saying to you I am saying to all; keep on the alert !'

The imagery in general is that of Jewish prophecy – the sun being darkened, the moon giving no light and the stars ceasing to shine. The image of 'the Son of Man coming in the clouds' is apparently taken directly from Daniel's vision (7:13) and foretells the coming of the kingdom of God in the midst of the cruel godless empires of this world.

It is exceedingly difficult to know what to make of this collection of sayings of Jesus. We do not know that they were all spoken at the same time nor do we know how far they are to be taken as picture-language. All we can be sure of is that Jesus is warning his disciples not to be deceived by false Christs and to remain steadfast in their faith to him. The end is to be the intervention of God in 'the human experiment' and Jesus is emphatic that his words are eternally true, even though he, the Son, does not know the day or the hour of the final consummation of human life on this planet. This is known only to the Father. Thus it would seem that this rather complex prophecy of Jesus does not end with the destruction of Jerusalem but is a picture of the suffering and persecution which will beset his followers to the end.

We live in an age when eventual human perfectibility is assumed, but the New Testament can be searched in vain for any such idea. It is true that the kingdom of God will spread throughout the world, but if we are to believe either Jesus or Paul as true prophets then the end of this age is the irruption of the timeless life of God into the life of time and space. This may be a million years from now or it may be tomorrow. Surely the point that both Jesus and Paul in his time are making is that the end of the human experiment depends on the action of God, which is both unknowable and unguessable by human minds. It is our job to remain alert and undiscouraged.

CHAPTER FOURTEEN

*

An act of love

vs 1–9 In two days' time the festival of the Passover and of unleavened bread was due. Consequently, the chief priests and the scribes were trying to think of some trick by which they could get Jesus into their power and have him executed.

'But it must not be during the festival,' they said, 'or there will be a riot.'

Jesus himself was now in Bethany in the house of Simon the leper. As he was sitting at table, a woman approached him with an alabaster flask of very costly spikenard perfume. She broke the neck of the flask and poured the perfume on Jesus' head. Some of those present were highly indignant and muttered,

'What is the point of such wicked waste of perfume? It could have been sold for over thirty pounds and the money given to the poor.' And there was a murmur of resentment against her. But Jesus said,

'Let her alone, why must you make her feel uncomfortable? She has done a beautiful thing for me. You have the poor with you always and you can do good to them whenever you like, but you will not always have me. She has done all she could – for she has anointed my body in preparation for burial. I assure you that wherever the gospel is preached throughout the whole world, this deed of hers will also be recounted, as her memorial to me.'

The Passover feast, which meant the ritual killing of lambs in the Temple and the feasting on them by households was by now closely connected with the ceremony of Unleavened Bread. The Jews would regard the old leaven as in some way symbolizing the sin of the past, and would begin by destroying all the old leaven and living on unleavened bread for several days. This rather lengthy festival was a yearly reminder of the time when the Jews were bidden to leave Egypt (Exodus 12 and Numbers 9). The unleavened bread was to remind them of the time when they were ordered to live on unfermented loaves for seven days in commemoration of their departure from Egypt (Exodus 23:15, Leviticus 23:6). Mark makes no mention of this slaying of the Passover lamb, but the complete Passover supper was a fairly complicated affair and needed careful preparation.

Before they move off to the Passover supper a woman not named by Matthew, Mark or Luke breaks an alabaster cruse of exceedingly expensive ointment and pours the contents over Jesus' head. We do not know why this was done and perhaps we may sympathize with the disciples' objection. Possibly through some kind of intuition the woman knew that Jesus was to die and was anointing his body in her attempt to make a gesture of memorial. Jesus plainly accepts this in the spirit in which it was made and will not allow her beautiful action to be spoiled by mundane considerations.

Judas volunteers to betray Jesus

vs 10, 11 Then Judas Iscariot, who was one of the twelve, went off to the chief priests to betray Jesus to them. And when they heard what he had to say, they were delighted and undertook to pay him money. So he looked for a convenient opportunity to betray him.

We do not quite know why this act of devotion should have prompted Judas to his first step on the road to treachery. Perhaps he is at last seeing that Jesus is not the kind of political Messiah for which he is hoping.

The Passover-supper prepared

vs 12–16 On the first day of unleavened bread, the day when the Passover was sacrificed, Jesus' disciples said to him,

'Where do you want us to go and make the preparations for you to eat the Passover?'

Jesus sent off two of them with these instructions,

'Go into the town and you will meet a man carrying a pitcher of water. Follow him and say to the owner of the house which he enters, "The Master says, where is the room for me to eat the Passover with my disciples?"

And he will show you a large upstairs room, set out and ready. That is where you must make our preparations.'

So the disciples set off and went into the town, found everything as he had told them, and prepared for the Passover.

It would seem probable that Jesus had already arranged for the place and the time for the Passover meal. Probably he had also planned for a man bearing a pitcher of water. This would have been an unusual sight, for carrying water was usually woman's work or the task of a slave. The preparations would entail the provision for thirteen people to recline on couches (the Jews did not at this time sit for their meals). There would also have to be the providing of the victim, the unleavened cakes, wine, water and bitter herbs which were used in the ceremony. It is a fascinating guess, though no more, that it was the house of Mary the mother of Mark which provided the room for the Passover meal. We know that she lived in or near Jerusalem and was a woman of some means and that her house was used as a meeting place for the early Christians (Acts 12:12). If she were responsible for making the preparations for the meal, what could be more natural than that she should ask her son Mark, who was probably only a youth at the time, to slip down and get her a pitcher of water.

The last supper together: the mysterious bread and wine

vs 17–28 Late in the evening he arrived with the twelve. And while they were sitting there, right in the middle of the meal, Jesus remarked,

'Believe me, one of you is going to betray me – someone who is now eating with me.'

This deeply distressed them and one after another they began to say to him,

'Surely, I'm not the one?'

'It is one of the twelve,' Jesus told them, 'a man who is dipping his hand into the dish with me. It is true that the Son of Man will follow the road foretold by the scriptures, but alas for the man through whom he is betrayed! It would be better for that man if he had never been born.'

And while they were still eating Jesus took a loaf, blessed it and broke it and gave it to them, with the words,

'Take this, it is my body.'

Then he took a cup, and after thanking God, he gave it to them, and they all drank from it, and he said to them,

'This is my blood of the new agreement, and it is shed for many. I tell you truly I will drink no more wine until the day comes when I drink it fresh in the kingdom of God!'

Then they sang a hymn and went out to the Mount of Olives.

'Every one of you will lose your faith in me,' Jesus told them, 'as the scripture says :

I will smite the shepherd,

And the sheep shall be scattered abroad.

Yet after I have risen, I shall go before you into Galilee!'

I think we may assume that Jesus observed the normal Jewish custom, and therefore to say that the one who was going to betray him would be one who dipped his hand into the dish with him would mean no more than that he was one of the small 'family' who were eating the meal together. No doubt the disciples were as mystified as they had been up till now by Jesus' statement that he was going to his death as the Old Testament had foretold. No doubt equally mysterious were the terrible words of condemnation pronounced upon the man who should prove to be the traitor.

The Passover ceremony was long and complicated, and we

cannot be sure at which point Jesus took the bread and said that it was 'his body', or the cup of wine which he gave them was 'his blood'. But they were surely used by now to his speaking in parables, and what must have struck them most was that it was a matter of a new covenant between God and man. It was not henceforth a matter of a sacrificial lamb and a drinking of the fruit of the vine but Jesus' actual giving of himself in sacramental form to reconcile man with God. Jesus is very emphatic that he will drink no more wine until he drinks it 'fresh in the kingdom of God'. This must surely mean that this is his last Passover on earth and that he will not drink wine again until he takes part in the feast of a better kind altogether when all things are made new. The hymn which they sang was probably what we know as Psalms 115–118.

After this they go out to what may well have been a garden. So great was the number of people assembled for the Passover festival that all such open spaces would be made available for the pilgrims. On the way to Gethsemane (which means oil-press) Jesus again prophesies the disaster which will befall him, quoting loosely from Zechariah 13:7. Undoubtedly Jesus is referring to his meeting them again in Galilee after the resurrection, but it is not at all sure that the disciples would so understand it.

Peter's bold words – and Jesus' reply

vs 29–31 Then Peter said to him,
'Even if everyone should lose his faith, I never will.'
'Believe me, Peter,' returned Jesus, 'this very night before the cock crows twice, you will disown me three times.'
But Peter protested violently,
'Even if it means dying with you, I will never disown you!'
And they all made the same protest.

When the disaster which Jesus continually prophesied was over they would naturally retreat to the parts of Galilee from which they had come. Jesus has already spoken of people being 'offended' or 'scandalized' but here he is telling his most intimate disciples that all of them will be similarly 'offended'. This is too much for Peter who cannot bear the thought of such cowardly unfaithfulness. He, at any rate, he declares, will never deny Jesus even if the price of faithfulness is death. He protests violently even though Jesus warns him that he will disown him three times before the cock crows twice. They all share in a vigorous protestation of faithfulness.

The last desperate prayer in Gethsemane

vs 32–42 Then they arrived at a place called Gethsemane, and Jesus said to his disciples,

'Sit down here while I pray.'

He took with him Peter, James and John, and began to be horror-stricken and desperately depressed.

'My heart is breaking with a death-like grief,' he told them. 'Stay here and keep watch.'

Then he walked forward a little way and flung himself on the ground, praying that, if it were possible, the hour might pass him by.

'Dear Father,' he said, 'all things are possible to you. Let me not have to drink this cup! Yet it is not what I want but what you want.'

Then he came and found them fast asleep. He spoke to Peter,

'Are you asleep, Simon? Couldn't you manage to stay awake for a single hour? Stay awake and pray, all of you, that you may not have to face temptation. Your spirit is willing, but human nature is weak.'

Then he went away again and prayed in the same words, and once more he came and found them asleep.

Then they arrived at a place called Gethsemane, and Jesus said to his disciples, 'Sit down here while I pray.' (Mark 14:32)

They could not keep their eyes open and they did not know what to say for themselves. When he came back for the third time, he said,

'Are you still going to sleep and take your ease? All right – the moment has come; now you will see the Son of Man betrayed into the hands of evil men! Get up, let us be going! Look, here comes my betrayer!'

When they come to Gethsemane Jesus leaves eight of the disciples outside the garden and takes with him only Peter, James and John. The others are to sit within calling distance. Mark can hardly find words to describe the terrifying inner conflict which immediately fell upon Jesus. He must be alone with his Father, and yet, naturally enough, he wants his friends to share something of his vigil. They would not have heard the whole of his agonized prayer, even if they had been awake to do so, but they might easily have heard the beginning of his desperate prayer. Both Abba and Father mean the same thing and could perhaps be best expressed in English by 'Dear Father'. Being a man, every fibre of Jesus' being would be crying out against not only the humiliation and torture which he knew would follow his arrest but against the intimate contact with evil which would be forced upon him. It is not too much to imagine that he senses that there is bound to be a terrible feeling of desolation and even apparent dereliction by his Father. Yet his whole life has been dedicated to doing his Father's will and he must not refuse to drink this last bitter cup. We can only guess at his desperate horror and agony of spirit. After a while he comes back to find Peter, James and John are fast asleep. Possibly in reproach he calls Peter by his old name of Simon and speaks to him by name as being the first to boast of his own loyalty. Before he goes away to pray again he urges them to pray too and especially to pray against temptation. Then he goes away and prays, at any rate at the beginning using the same words, and again after an interval, he comes back to find them unable to keep

awake. He begins to ask them a question and then, possibly
out of the corner of his eye, he sees the armed band who have
come to arrest him. The word I have translated 'all right' is
difficult. Literally it means 'enough'. I have tried to express
the suddenness with which Jesus realizes that the situation
has now completely changed, and that he is prepared to face
it. Let them at least get to their feet and walk forwards
towards the armed mob which the chief priests, scribes and
elders had assembled.

Judas betrays Jesus

vs 43–52 And suddenly, while the words were still on
his lips, Judas, one of the twelve, arrived with a mob
armed with swords and staves, sent by the chief priests
and scribes and elders. The betrayer had given them a
sign; he had said, 'The one I kiss will be the man. Get
hold of him and you can take him away without any
trouble.' So he walked straight up to Jesus, cried,
'Master!' and kissed him affectionately. And so they got
hold of him and held him. Somebody present drew his
sword and struck at the High Priest's servant, slashing off
his ear. Then Jesus spoke to them,

'So you've come out with your swords and staves
to capture me like a bandit, have you? Day after day
I was with you in the Temple, teaching, and you
never laid a finger on me. But the scriptures must be
fulfilled.'

Then all the disciples deserted him and made their
escape. There happened to be a young man among
Jesus' followers who wore nothing but a linen shirt. They
seized him, but he left the shirt in their hands and took
to his heels stark naked.

Judas, who knew where they would be likely to spend the
night, comes forward and gives what would be a normal

salute to a rabbi, a kiss. This was the prearranged signal and Jesus was at once arrested. In the confusion someone draws his sword and slashes off the high priest's servant's ear. But Jesus does not intend the struggle to become this kind of undignified scuffle in the half-dark. He faces them boldly, and asks them scathingly why they have waited until now. For several days now he has been teaching in the Temple completely unarmed. But the scriptures and prophecies, particularly such passages as Isaiah 53, are all part of God's plan and must be fulfilled.

At this point all the disciples make their escape. The curious incident of the young man dressed in the linen shirt, occurs only in this Gospel. It is a guess, but only a guess, that the youth was Mark himself. It has no relevance to the main story, but if Mark were writing the Gospel with Peter it would certainly be the kind of incident he would never have forgotten and would feel bound to record.

Jesus before the High Priest

vs 53–65 So they marched Jesus away to the High Priest in whose presence all the chief priests and elders and scribes had assembled. (Peter followed him at a distance, right into the High Priest's courtyard. There he sat in the firelight with the servants, keeping himself warm.) Meanwhile, the chief priests and the whole council were trying to find some evidence against Jesus which would warrant the death penalty. But they failed completely. There were plenty of people ready to give false testimony against him, but their evidence was contradictory. Then some more perjurers stood up and said,

'We heard him say, "I will destroy this Temple that was built by human hands and in three days I will build another made without human aid." '

But even so their evidence conflicted. So the High Priest himself got up and took the centre of the floor.

'Have you no answer to make?' he asked Jesus. 'What about all this evidence against you?'

But Jesus remained silent and offered no reply. Again the High Priest asked him,

'Are you Christ, Son of the blessed one?'

And Jesus said,

'I am! Yes, you will see the Son of Man sitting at the right hand of power, coming in the clouds of heaven.'

Then the High Priest tore his robes and cried,

'Why do we still need witnesses? You heard the blasphemy; what is your opinion now?'

Their unanimous verdict was that he deserved to die. Then some of them began to spit at him. They blindfolded him and then smacked him, saying,

'Now prophesy who hit you!'

Even the servants who took him away slapped his face.

The enemies of Jesus have now to work fast if their whole murderous scheme is to be carried through before the Sabbath. It would seem probable that the assembly of 'all the chief priests and elders and scribes' had been prearranged. Caiaphas is probably the high priest referred to and it is to his residence that Jesus is taken. The rooms of the residence would have been built round a courtyard and here there is a charcoal fire burning. The Levitical guards and very possibly some of the ordinary people would have crowded in for the sake of the warmth. Peter undoubtedly hoped to make his way inside without being recognized. Only Mark mentions that he was warming himself *by the light* of the fire. Within the building itself a confused mockery of a trial took place. Feelings ran high and no two witnesses agreed in their testimony, a requirement of the Mosaic Law where a capital offence was concerned. They even seem to have muddled Jesus' prophecy about the destruction of the Temple. For Jesus did not say that he himself would destroy the Temple, nor did he say that he would build another one in three days without human

labour. Caiaphas appears to be unimpressed with what seems
to him a badly put together case, especially as Jesus makes
no attempt to defend himself. So he is driven to ask the direct
question as to whether Jesus was Christ 'the Son of the blessed
one', a title unmistakable in its meaning but only found in
Mark. At this Jesus breaks his silence and asserts that he is,
and that the Son of Man would come to judge in power.
(The actual words used by Jesus recall Daniel 7:13 and
Psalm 110 which were commonly interpreted in a Messianic
sense.) To claim to be the Messiah and the Son of God was
the crowning blasphemy and to the Jews called for the death
penalty. It would appear that the Jews were not allowed to
carry out the death penalty themselves, which would have
been by stoning, but they could refer a case which they
considered deserving of the penalty of death to the Roman
authorities. And so it was decided, and in the interval that it
took officially to inform the Romans a spate of insult and
abuse broke upon Jesus. Those who indulged in these sordid
cruelties would have been members of the Sanhedrin themselves, the guard who arrested Jesus and the attendants of the
Sanhedrin.

Peter, in fear, disowns his master

vs 66–72 In the meantime, while Peter was in the courtyard below, one of the High Priest's maids came and saw
him warming himself. She looked closely at him, and
said,

'You were with the Nazarene too – with Jesus!'

But he denied it, saying,

'I neither know nor understand what you're talking
about.'

And he walked out into the gateway, and a cock crew.

Then the maid who had noticed him began to say
again to the men standing there,

'This man is one of them!'

But he denied it again. A few minutes later the bystanders themselves said to Peter,

'You certainly are one of them. Why, you're a
Galilean!'

But he started to curse and swear, saying,

'I tell you I don't know the man you're talking about!'

Immediately the cock crew for the second time, and
back into Peter's mind came the words of Jesus, 'Before
the cock crows twice, you will disown me three times.'

And as the truth broke upon him he burst into tears.

Now follows the unhappy story of Peter's denial. After his
first denial of any knowledge of Jesus and his affairs Peter
leaves the bright light of the fire and goes out into the porch.
But the serving maid or slave girl was not satisfied and accuses
him again, only to be met by a further denial. But the story
begins to grow and one of the bystanders says that Peter is
certainly a Galilean, probably by reason of his accent. By now
Peter is at the end of his tether and he reverts to the coarse
swearing of the fisherman he once was. At the third denial the
cock crows a second time and Peter remembers Jesus' words
and as the contrast between his own protests of bravery and his
actual acts of cowardice break upon him he bursts into tears.

CHAPTER FIFTEEN

*

Jesus before Pilate

vs 1–21 The moment daylight came the chief priests
called together a meeting of elders, scribes and the whole
council. They bound Jesus and took him off and handed
him over to Pilate. Pilate asked him straight out,

'Well, you – *are* you the king of the Jews?'

'You say that I am,' he replied.

The chief priests brought many accusations. So Pilate questioned him again,

'Have you nothing to say? Listen to all their accusations!'

But Jesus made no further answer – to Pilate's astonishment.

Now it was Pilate's custom at festival-time to release a prisoner – anyone they asked for. There was in the prison at the time, with some other rioters who had committed murder in a recent revolt, a man called Barabbas. The crowd surged forward and began to demand that Pilate should do what he usually did for them. So he spoke to them,

'Do you want me to set free the king of the Jews for you?'

For he knew perfectly well that the chief priests had handed Jesus over to him through sheer malice. But the chief priests worked upon the crowd to get them to release Barabbas rather than Jesus. So Pilate addressed them once more,

'Then what am I to do with the man whom you call the king of the Jews?'

They shouted back,

'Crucify him!'

But Pilate replied,

'Why, what crime has he committed?'

But their voices rose to a roar,

'Crucify him!'

And as Pilate wanted to satisfy the crowd, he set Barabbas free for them, and after having Jesus flogged handed him over to be crucified.

Then the soldiers marched him away inside the courtyard of the governor's residence and called their whole company together. They dressed Jesus in a purple robe, and twisting some thorn-twigs into a crown, they put it on his head. Then they began to salute him,

'Hail, your majesty – king of the Jews!'

They hit him on the head with a stick and spat at him, and then bowed low before him on bended knee. And when they had finished their fun with him, they took off the purple cloak and dressed him again in his own clothes. Then they led him outside to crucify him. They compelled Simon, a native of Cyrene in Africa (the father of Alexander and Rufus), who was on his way from the fields at the time, to carry Jesus' cross.

The feast has now begun and the risk of a popular outbreak in favour of Jesus is great. The chief priests and others get Jesus brought before the Roman authority as early as they can. Roman courts never opened before sunrise, and the time is now probably 5 or 6 am. Pilate wastes no time but asks the direct question. The reply of Jesus is an affirmative one and would be so understood by those familiar with Greek usage. To translate literally 'you say so' is to make the simple answer too subtle and indirect. Then follows a torrent of accusations from the chief priests but Jesus makes no reply. Pilate is not given a very good character by writers outside the New Testament, but what he wants to establish is first whether Jesus is making a claim to be king, which is seditious, and to give him an opportunity to make a reply. This was the normal Roman course of justice. Since Jesus makes no reply, and possibly because Pilate is not altogether easy in his own conscience, for he can sense that Jesus has been brought to him through sheer malice, he thinks of a possible solution. It was apparently the custom for him to release a prisoner for them at Passover time, and he thinks of Barabbas, at this moment lying bound in prison awaiting execution. We know nothing of this man, but he may have enjoyed a temporary popularity among the mob for taking part in an insurrection against the hated Romans. Indeed the crowds began to call for their privilege and for this particular rogue to be released. Even now Pilate does not believe that this is their real desire and has the good sense to see that the crowd are acting under the influence of the malice of their leaders. But his last effort to get Jesus released fails, for the chief priests persuade the people to insist that Barabbas shall be released, and Jesus crucified. Mark makes no mention of the incident recorded by Matthew of Pilate's publicly washing his hands to show that he personally was innocent of the death of Jesus. Nevertheless the general feeling of this short passage is that Pilate is doing his best in a very difficult situation to avoid sentencing an innocent man to death. But he fails, releases Barabbas, and has Jesus flogged. A Roman flogging was such a terrible infliction of pain that quite frequently the victim died from its effects.

The rough horseplay of the Roman soldiers, revolting as it was, sounds very probable. The soldiers do not every day have a prisoner making himself out to be king and they make the most of it.

Jesus is now physically exhausted and is unable to carry the crossbar of the cross which normally a condemned prisoner was required to bear to the place of execution. This is no problem to the Romans for they had the power to 'compel' or 'impress' ordinary civilians to carry out manual tasks. It may be that Alexander and Rufus were known to the early Church and that is why Mark mentions their father's action.

The crucifixion

vs 22–41 They took him to a place called Golgotha (which means Skull Hill) and they offered him some drugged wine, but he would not take it. Then they crucified him, and shared out his garments, drawing lots to see what each of them would get. It was nine o'clock in the morning when they nailed him to the cross. Over his head the placard of his crime read, 'THE KING OF THE JEWS.' They also crucified two bandits at the same time, one on each side of him. And the passers-by jeered at him, shaking their heads in mockery, saying,

'Hi, you! You could destroy the Temple and build it up again in three days, why not come down from the cross and save yourself?'

The chief priests also made fun of him among themselves and the scribes, and said,

'He saved others, he cannot save himself. If only this Christ, the king of Israel, would come down from the cross, we should see it and believe!'

And even the men who were crucified with him hurled abuse at him.

At midday darkness spread over the whole countryside and lasted until three o'clock in the afternoon, and at three o'clock Jesus cried out in a loud voice,

'My God, my God, why did you forsake me?'

Some of the bystanders heard these words which Jesus spoke in Aramaic (*Eloi, Eloi, lama sabachthani?*), and said,

'Listen, he's calling for Elijah!'

One man ran off and soaked a sponge in vinegar, put it on a stick, and held it up for Jesus to drink, calling out,

'Let him alone! Let's see if Elijah will come and take him down!'

But Jesus let out a great cry, and expired. The curtain of the Temple sanctuary was split in two from the top to the bottom. And when the centurion who stood in front of Jesus saw how he died, he said,

'This man was certainly a son of God!'

There were some women there looking on from a distance, among them Mary of Magdala, Mary the mother of the younger James and Joses, and Salome. These were the women who used to follow Jesus as he went about in Galilee and look after him. And there were many other women there who had come up to Jerusalem with him.

All executions took place outside the city, possibly at the roadside so that as many as possible could see what happened to those who set themselves up against the power of Rome. We do not know why Jesus refused to take their drugged wine that was customarily offered to those who were to undergo the agony of crucifixion. It may be because of his promise at the last supper that he would drink no more wine until he drank it new in the kingdom. Or it may be that Jesus is prepared to accept the total agony of crucifixion without alleviation. It was customary for the soldiers to share out the garments of men who were crucified.

Mark alone mentions this particular time for the crucifixion. The discrepancy between this account and John's may be because Mark was using the Jewish divisions of time and John, who says it was 'about the sixth hour', was using the Roman divisions of time. If this is so, they would both mean that the crucifixion took place early in the morning.

It was customary for the crime of the crucified man to be nailed over his head and in this case of course the chief crime is that of making himself out to be King of the Jews. The two bandits who were crucified at the same time may have been guerilla fighters, part of Barabbas' party perhaps, or they may have been ordinary highway robbers. The mockery of the crowd is understandable, but it makes painful reading. The chief priests could not restrain their own mockery, even though it was not public. Jesus' fellow-sufferers join in the general derision. It is in Luke's account that we read that only one of them joined in such contempt, but it is from Luke too that we learn that the soldiers themselves, to whom crucifixion was a common enough sight, added their abuse.

This sudden darkness caused by a sandstorm is not uncommon in some parts of the world and one of the frightening things about it is that one has no knowledge of how long it is going to last. It can be accompanied by a fierce wind and could be responsible for the tearing of the veil before the Holy of Holies in the Temple. It could not have been an ordinary eclipse since the moon was 'full' at Passion-time.

The quotation at the end of the period of three hours of darkness is from Psalm 22 and was shouted in a loud voice. I do not myself believe that Jesus made his great cry in the midst of his agony of body and spirit, but when the worst part, the separation from his Father, had passed. That is why I have translated it as a question referring to the immediate past and not to the present. The words in Aramaic sound to bystanders roughly like a cry for Elijah.

One of the peculiar tortures of crucifixion was the appalling thirst which it produced. One of the bystanders held up a sponge soaked in the rough wine of the soldiers for Jesus to drink. Whether it was this man or another of the bystanders who made the next remark we don't know. But before Jesus could, even if he would, accept such relief he cried out in a loud voice and died. The implication is that this was no feeble whimper of a totally exhausted man but a great shout, possibly even of triumph, and he deliberately handed back his spirit to his Father.

The centurion had no doubt seen many men die but there was something special in the way Jesus gave up his spirit. Exactly what the centurion's remark meant we do not know. It certainly was not a theological statement but it may well be that the soldier recognized that this was the death of some-one extraordinary. Possibly he had read the placard over Jesus' head and felt that the claim that Jesus had made was, in some degree, true.

Other witnesses of the actual death of Jesus were Mary from Magdala, Mary the mother of James (the less or the little) and Joses. The name Salome was borne by several members of the Herodian household. There were also other women who had followed Jesus to Jerusalem to be near him at his tragic end.

The body of Jesus is reverently laid in a tomb

vs 42–47 When the evening came, because it was the day of preparation, that is the day before the Sabbath, Joseph from Arimathea, a distinguished member of the council, who was himself prepared to accept the kingdom of God, went with great courage into Pilate's presence and asked for the body of Jesus. Pilate was surprised that he could be dead already and he sent for the centurion and asked whether he had been dead long. On hearing the centurion's report, he gave Joseph the body of Jesus. So Joseph brought a linen winding-sheet, took Jesus down and wrapped him in it, and then put him in a tomb which had been hewn out of the solid rock, rolling a stone over the entrance to it. Mary of Magdala and Mary the mother of Joses were looking on and saw where he was laid.

Now, with considerable courage, Joseph of Arimathea, a man of some distinction in the Sanhedrin, comes forward and asks Pilate for the body of Jesus. Normally the bodies of the crucified were left hanging in the sun and rain open to the attacks of predators. The more merciful Jewish Law ordered that the body of one executed should not be left exposed but buried on the day of hanging or crucifixion (Deuteronomy 21:23). Those who were crucified sometimes lingered for a day or more and Pilate was surprised that Jesus was already dead, and it is not until he has ascertained from the centurion that this is so that he makes a present of the corpse to Joseph.

According to John's account Nicodemus assists Joseph to remove the body of Jesus and to add aromatic spices in the folds of the linen cloth which Joseph has provided. The body was put into a stone-hewn tomb (according to Matthew, Joseph's own) and the customary large stone rolled down its slot to close the door of the tomb. Two women, according to Mark, saw where the body was laid.

CHAPTER SIXTEEN

*

Early on the first Lord's day: the women are amazed

vs 1–8 When the Sabbath was over, Mary of Magdala, Mary the mother of James, and Salome bought spices so that they could go and anoint him. And very early in the morning on the first day of the week, they came to the tomb, just as the sun was rising.

'Who is going to roll the stone back from the doorway of the tomb?' they asked each other.

And then as they looked closer, they saw that the stone, which was a very large one, had been rolled back. So they went into the tomb and saw a young man in a white robe sitting on the right-hand side, and they were simply astonished. But he said to them,

'There is no need to be astonished. You are looking for Jesus of Nazareth who was crucified. He has risen; he is not here. Look, here is the place where they laid him. But now go and tell his disciples, and Peter, that he will be in Galilee before you. You will see him there just as he told you.'

And they got out of the tomb and ran away from it. They were trembling with excitement. They did not dare to breathe a word to anyone.

The Sabbath is now over and the two Marys and Salome buy spices and return to the tomb to complete the work of embalming. The day is beginning to break and the sun has in fact risen by the time they get to the tomb. By now it is light enough for them to see that the problem which had been puzzling them has been solved. The very large stone has been

138

rolled back and the tomb is open. Naturally enough they go into the tomb and there they see a young man dressed in white sitting on the right-hand side. They are amazed to the point of terror, but the young man who is an angel of God, and not to be confused with the cherubic-faced angels of much church illustration, tells them there is no need for their fear or astonishment. Jesus whom they have been looking for is not here, as they can see. Then they are instructed to go and tell his disciples including Peter, despite his three-fold denial, that Jesus would meet them in Galilee as he had promised. The women run from the tomb, they are trembling with excitement and do not dare to speak a word to anyone.

This is where Mark's Gospel really ends and the verses which follow have been added at a later date. Whether Mark meant to end on this note of amazement and fear we simply do not know, and of course it is possible that the end of the manuscript was somehow lost. It has even been suggested that because of the urgent and terrifying persecution which was beginning to bear down upon all Christians, Mark was not able to write any more. At any rate it is universally agreed that the rest of the chapter was written by another hand.

An ancient appendix

vs 9–18 When Jesus rose early on that first day of the week, he appeared first of all to Mary of Magdala, from whom he had driven out seven evil spirits. And she went and reported this to his sorrowing and weeping followers. They heard her say that he was alive and that she had seen him, but they did not believe it.

Later, he appeared in a different form to two of them who were out walking, as they were on their way to the country. These two came back and told the others, but they did not believe them either. Still later he appeared to the eleven themselves as they were sitting at table and reproached them for their lack of faith and refusal to believe those who had seen him after he had risen. Then he said to them,

'You must go out to the whole world and proclaim the gospel to every creature. He who believes it and is baptized will be saved, but he who disbelieves it will be condemned. These signs will follow those who do believe: they will drive out evil spirits in my name; they will speak with new tongues; they will pick up snakes, and if they drink any poison it will do them no harm; they will lay their hands upon the sick and they will recover.'

The appendix above is not written in the style of Mark. Nevertheless it was accepted from early times as a genuine addition written by an early disciple with the Church's authority.

It would appear that someone felt that there should be some 'bridging', however short, between the scene of the bewildered and frightened women and the Church now extending her work by the power of God in all parts of the world.

The first appearance was to Mary Magdalene but her story was not believed. We may compare this with Luke's account where the reports of the women were regarded as 'sheer imagination' (Luke 24:11). The eleven were so sunk in despair and sorrow that they were unable to believe. The news was too good to be true. Even the appearance of Jesus 'in a different form' (meaning perhaps only 'looking different') to the two on their walk to Emmaus is not accepted as true. Luke 24:30–35, however, tells us that their story *was* accepted, and that Jesus had already appeared to Peter.

According to this account it is only now that Jesus appears to the assembled apostles, and rebukes them for their refusal to believe. Then he turns the rebuke into a command to take the Gospel into the whole world, and promises special powers to those who go forth in his name.

Jesus, his mission accomplished, returns to Heaven

vs 19, 20 After these words to them, the Lord Jesus was taken up into Heaven and was enthroned at the right hand of God. They went out and preached everywhere. The Lord worked with them, confirming their message by the signs that followed.

There is no need to assume that there is no time interval between this commission and the ascension itself. It must have been widely known that the early believers had to wait in Jerusalem for the promised 'power'; and that it was not until the Holy Spirit was given so publicly and so powerfully that the young Church moved out into the world, 'the Lord working with them'.

THE
FIRST LETTER OF
PETER

CHAPTER ONE

*

vs 1–12 Peter, a messenger of Jesus Christ, sends this letter to God's people now dispersed in Pontus, Galatia, Cappadocia, Asia and Bithynia, whom God the Father knew and chose long ago to be made holy by his Spirit, that they might obey Jesus Christ and be cleansed by his blood : may you know more and more of God's grace and peace.

Your faith is being tested, but your future is magnificent

vs 3–12 Thank God, the God and Father of our Lord Jesus Christ, that in his great mercy we have been born again into a life full of hope, though Christ's rising again from the dead! You can now hope for a perfect inheritance beyond the reach of change and decay, reserved in Heaven for you. And in the meantime you are guarded by the power of God operating through your faith, till you enter fully into the salvation which is all ready to be revealed at the last. This means tremendous joy to you, even though at present you may be temporarily harassed by all kinds of trials. This is no accident – it happens to prove your faith, which is infinitely more valuable than gold, and gold, as you know, even though it is ultimately perishable, must be purified by fire. This proving of your faith is planned to result in praise and glory and honour in the day when Jesus Christ reveals himself. And though you have never seen him, yet you love him. At present you trust him without being able to see him, and even now he brings you a joy that words cannot express and which has in it a hint of the glories of Heaven; and all the time you are receiving the result of your faith in him – the salvation of your own souls. The prophets of old did their utmost to discover and obtain this salvation. They prophesied of this grace that has now come to you. They tried hard to discover to what time and to what sort of circumstances the Spirit of Christ working in them was referring. For they foretold the sufferings of Christ and the glories that should follow them. It was then made clear to them that they were dealing with matters not meant for themselves, but for you. It is these very matters which have been made plain to you by those who preached the gospel to you by the Holy Spirit sent from Heaven – and these are facts to command the interest of the very angels!

Peter is a messenger in a special sense; he is an *Apostle*. The word means no more than 'one who is sent', but by the time of the writing of this letter it was well known throughout the rapidly expanding Church to mean one personally chosen by Jesus Christ, and sent by him.

Some have raised difficulties about the good Greek used in this letter. 'How could the rough fisherman,' they ask, somewhat naïvely, 'use a language so well and so skilfully?' They seem to forget that Peter was by no means a stupid man. He has by now had over thirty years to improve his knowledge of the language. Almost everyone spoke the Koine, the common day-to-day Greek. It is surely possible that a man filled with a passion to communicate the message, and the love of his Lord, should have rapidly acquired a facility in an almost universal language. Of course, when it came to the actual writing of this letter, he may have had help from people such as Silvanus (5:12); why not?

Peter is writing to a wide audience spread over an enormous area. Pontus and Bithynia are districts on the southern shores of what is now called the Black Sea. Cappadocia, Galatia and Asia are large provinces in what we nowadays call Asia Minor. All are under Roman control. All these Christian groups, naturally, owe their existence to the strenuous journeyings and unceasing labour of some Apostles and ministers over the last thirty years. Surely this is not merely a superhuman but a miraculous piece of human history.

To tell men and women such things as 'whom God the Father knew and chose long ago to be made holy by his Spirit' is in any man's eyes revolutionary to an almost incredible degree. To the Jews who believed such privileges to be their own 'monopoly', it was the most outrageous blasphemy. Here, and everywhere throughout the New Testament epistles, this new message is given with complete conviction. It is indeed Good News.

To obey Jesus Christ is man's part in response to this revolutionary declaration; to be cleansed by his blood is God's. (The original idea of 'cleansing by sprinkling' goes back a long way; see Exodus 24:8.)

God's 'grace' (Greek, *charis*) here means the operation of his love and power in human life; his peace may be interpreted as widely as we like. The people to whom this letter is addressed knew something of these things. Peter's wish is that their experience may be multiplied many times.

'Born again': an expression immensely popular with many modern evangelists occurs only once in the Gospels (John 3:1–11) when Jesus speaks to a particular person in a specialized situation. Nevertheless Nicodemus, who has been addressed in the singular, is then suddenly met with a plural verb: 'you (plural) must be born again.' This must surely mean that 'people like you' (the righteous and religious) need a new birth to appreciate the kingdom of God. Jesus, in his wide and varied contacts with men and women, never used such an expression to anyone else. Is there a contradiction here? Of course not. As the young Church grew, thousands and thousands came to leave the darkness and ignorance of their past and put their faith in Christ. Both to them and to those who prayerfully watched them, this step resulted in such a fundamental change that it felt like a new birth and gave every outward appearance of the same. Thus we find throughout the New Testament letters many instances of the idea of re-birth or new birth.

It happens today, thank God. Usually not so dramatically, for we are a country steeped in 1500 years of Christianity, but suddenly or gradually it still happens.

The human being who is 'born again' in Christ is now indissolubly linked with the timeless life and limitless resource of God. On earth he experiences something enormously real and valuable, but it is only the foretaste of the perfect inheritance reserved in Heaven. Today's world is interested only in this world; the Christian possesses infinitely more, both in hope and resources.

Meantime, to maintain this conviction in a Godless and corrupt world is difficult. It would be impossible if the power of God not did guard the individual Christian; and this becomes practical through the faith of the believer. He is only at the beginning of his 'salvation', which is regarded as a process throughout the New Testament. After earthly 'death' the same salvation expands and accelerates in love and light and knowledge – and all things good.

'Tremendous joy'? The New Testament rings with it but how far do we know it? Is it possible that we listen too much to this world, to its crazy values and priorities? Because it is near and noisy are we cheated of our joy in the guaranteed future? 'Harassed by all kinds of trials'. Indeed the early Christians were! But I have never met a Christian of today, young or old, who is not being 'harassed', widely as their trials appear to vary in nature or severity. We are in good company.

'No accident'. Life has always been hard, unfair, risky, frightening, painful and to very many a heavy burden. The Christian does not avoid any ordinary human pains and trials and he is bound, if he is faithful to Christ, to experience something of the bitter conflict that first showed itself in the life and death of the man Jesus. There is not today much physical danger in being a Christian in this country; but there is in many. Nevertheless, frightening pressures may wound any Christian anywhere; pressures from an evil world, pressures from his own primitive unredeemed nature, and pressures from the powers of evil. Yet 'this is no accident'! Sooner or later, and naturally the sooner the better, the Christian has to accept this cheerfully. Nothing less than the power of God can enable us to accept, to persist and to endure.

The high mysterious purpose of all this is the purifying of our faith. Often it appears purposeless and even cruel. We feel we cannot take any more. No matter what our feelings tell us we must hold on. Faith may have to continue in darkness, even in seeming desolation. But, as Jesus himself said, 'he that endures to the end shall be saved.' The 'end-product' is promised in the last words of verse 7.

We may feel 'how easy for Peter, who saw Jesus almost daily for a few years!' But was it easy, for him or for any of the contemporaries of Jesus? The four Gospels will give us the answer. The concern is always with the present and with the magnificent future; almost never with the past.

It is surely a miracle, a top-ranking miracle, that all these people, scattered over many thousands of square miles, should love someone they had never seen. Over the years I have met thousands of twentieth-century people who have never seen him, but love him. Certainly this is a miracle of today and a very impressive one. Hints and hopes of the glories to come as well as a super-worldly joy come to all Christians, to some constantly, to others only intermittently.

'All the time' the process of 'salvation' is going on, quietly and unseen – irrespective of what our wayward thoughts and feelings are doing.

The Old Testament prophets – this term would include prophetic words in the Psalms as well – had indeed their 'inklings' and their intuition. They were completely open on the Godward side and in many years of meditation and contemplation each has his special vision and message. With the benefit of hindsight we can naturally (and no credit to us) see what it is they were groping for or hinting at. Sometimes, one feels they saw the truth clearly, but there is little time-sense and they did not know the *when* of their inspired words.

'Sufferings of Christ'. See Psalm 22 and Isaiah 53 especially. If a 'reference Bible' is available it would be most useful here, directing us to similar or parallel passages elsewhere. See also Hebrews 2:12–18.

'Angels'. They occur fairly frequently in the New Testament. Traditionally they knew something of God's secret purposes, and were sinless dwellers in Heaven. Man, 'a little lower than the angels', has now a full understanding of God's purpose – insofar as his human limitations allow.

Consider soberly what God has done for you

vs 13–21 So brace up your minds, and, as men who know what they are doing, rest the full weight of your hopes on the grace that will be yours when Jesus Christ reveals himself. Live as obedient children before God. Don't let your character be moulded by the desires of your ignorant days, but be holy in every part of your lives, for the one who has called you is himself holy. The scripture says:

Ye shall be holy; for I am holy.

If you pray to a Father who judges men by their actions without the slightest favouritism, then you should spend the time of your stay here on earth with reverent fear. For you must realize that you have been ransomed from the futile way of living passed on to you by your traditions, but not by any money payment of this passing world. No, the price was in fact the life-blood of Christ, the unblemished and unstained lamb of sacrifice. It is true that he was destined for this purpose before the

world was founded, but it was for your benefit that he
was revealed in these last days – for you who found your
faith in God through him. And God raised him from the
dead and gave him heavenly splendour, so that all your
faith and hope might be centred in God.

Verse 13 has been rather freely translated, and calls for
revision, I think. Better than 'brace up your minds' would be
'let your minds be stripped for action'. (I owe this thought to
Dr William Barclay's translation.)

Because you have been privileged to know God's plan and
given some idea of a shining future promised to you, *therefore*
you must do your part in mental and spiritual discipline.
Faith must be total and hope also, both now and in the
magnificent promises of timeless life to come.

This phrase, 'your ignorant days', would never have been
used to Jewish Christians. No Jew lived in ignorance; he knew
as much as he could in the days of the Law and the Prophets.
Such knowledge was incomplete, and was now superseded.
The Gentiles (assorted pagans of various religions) had hitherto spent their days in ignorance, and quite suddenly see a new
God, a new Lord and Saviour and experience a new Spirit.
Life is transformed; values, aims and ideals are utterly
different. There must be a complete break with old ideas and
a total concentration on being 'holy'. Holy has become to us
a rather unreal and off-putting word. It is a hard word to
translate; it means, 'whole, healthy, pure, dedicated, separate
and consecrated to God, and thus owing no loyalty to the
world's value-systems' and much else. Here, and indeed for us
today, the meaning is to be 'holy' as Christ was, and is, holy.
The re-direction of life, which involves continual checking,
teaching and guidance from the Spirit who lives in us, is
always in the direction of making us holy. We can see real
true holiness in the four Gospels, as well as in such classic
passages as 1 Corinthians 13.

Peter naturally quotes the Old Testament (Leviticus 11:45

and *passim* in the Old Testament) to reinforce his words. We
may not feel the need of such support, but it is at least
strengthening to reflect that God's purpose for man, though
gradually revealed, is consistent and changeless.

You may now, writes Peter, confidently call God 'Father',
(Jesus taught this and so, of course, did Paul again and again.
See Romans 8:15.) But though you are now 'sons' there is
no place for familiarity in this high calling. There must be no
taking advantage of the position, no feeling of being so safe
and privileged that you can 'do your own thing' regardless
of God.

There is a further and very cogent reason for reverent fear.
You have been 'ransomed', and at fearful and infinite cost.
We may be left quite cold by the form of this thought today,
for we hardly live in a world of ransoms – except in criminally
wicked situations. Whether children, businessmen, bank staff
or politicians are kidnapped or held captive, they are held
until certain demands, usually for money, but sometimes for
personal or political gain, are met. They are thus prisoners
until the 'ransom' is paid. But in the ancient world ransom was
a most important and often vital word. Prisoners were ransomed, and slaves sometimes set free, usually by payment in
gold or silver. The released were naturally grateful, sometimes
very grateful, but they did not usually feel that the rest of
their lives must be lived in utter devotion to their benefactor;
unless of course they were ransomed at the cost of another
man's life.

The case of the Christian is on a much higher level. The
price of his 'ransom' (Mark 10:45) is nothing less than the
'blood' or 'life' of Christ. This is no place for theories of atonement or reconciliation between God and man. The New
Testament is unanimous that the cost of it was beyond the
highest human thought or endeavour. The fact that 'God
was in Christ reconciling the world unto himself' (2 Corinthians 5:19) can only be humbly and gratefully accepted.
This is as true today as it was then.

It is impossible for those who have been 'ransomed' or 'redeemed' from all the errors of false thinking of the past to exploit their new freedom for selfish or evil ends.

'Destined' might be misunderstood. It means that God, whose knowledge is infinite, knew the complexity of the problem and its solution before the world began. Man has a great deal of freedom; he is not *fated*, yet at all times moves within the timeless plan of God. The plan is revealed to all who open their lives, minds, hearts and spirits – their total personality – to the living Christ. They find faith in God through him.

'Last days' means literally 'the end of the times'. Only God knows when the human experiment will end, but compared with the millions of years since life began on this planet surely it is allowable to think that we live in 'the last days'. The historical guarantee of the truth of all this lies in the death and 'raising' of Christ. All truths, large and small, are ultimately subservient to this act of God in human life.

Let your life match your high calling

vs 22–25 Now that you have, by obeying the truth, made your souls clean enough for a genuine love of your fellows, see that you do love each other, fervently and from the heart. For you are not just mortals now but sons of God; the live, permanent Word of the living God has given you his own indestructible heredity.

It is true that :

All flesh is as grass,

And all the glory thereof as the flower of grass.

The grass withereth, and the flower falleth :

But the word of the Lord abideth for ever.

The Word referred to is the message of the gospel that was preached to you.

All human beings have some measure of love, however lowly,

restricted or distorted. No one can know pure love except by the refining and inspiration of God's Spirit. We are to love like this in purity and with great warmth. With God 'all things are possible'; even this transforming of our own partial, and rather mixed-up, love.

'Heredity'. See 1 John 3:1–3. The guarantee of the new position is God's unchanging Word.

All human activity is doomed to destruction. What God says is alone permanent and unchanging.

CHAPTER TWO

*

vs 1–10 Have done, then, with all evil and deceit, all pretence and jealousy and slander. You are babies, new-born in God's family, and you should be crying out for unadulterated spiritual milk to make you grow up to salvation! And so you will, if you have already tasted the goodness of the Lord.

You have come to the living Stone despised indeed by men but chosen and greatly honoured by God. So you yourselves, as living stones, must be built up into a spiritual House of God, in which you become a holy priesthood, able to offer those spiritual sacrifices which are acceptable to God by Jesus Christ. There is a passage to this effect in scripture, and it runs like this:

Behold I lay in Zion a chief corner stone, elect, precious:

And he that believeth on him shall not be put to shame. It is to you that believe in him that he is 'precious', but to those who disobey God, it is true that:

The stone which the builders rejected,

The same was made the head of the corner.

And he is, to them,

A stone of stumbling and a rock of offence.

Yes, they stumble at the Word of God for in their hearts they are unwilling to obey it – which makes stumbling a foregone conclusion. But you are God's 'chosen generation', his 'royal priesthood', his 'holy nation', his 'peculiar people' – all the old titles of God's people now belong to you. It is for you now to demonstrate the goodness of him who has called you out of darkness into his amazing light. In the past you were not 'a people' at all : now you are the people of God. In the past you had no experience of his mercy, but now it is intimately yours.

'Have done'. This means a deliberate act of putting aside all dishonest and self-centred human emotions. To pretend that they aren't there would be further dishonesty; but by the power of Christ they can be daily denied, though the process for most of us may last for many years.

Truth to be absorbed like mother's milk was a fairly common metaphor to the Jews and sometimes to the Greeks. It is rather a strange thought to many Christians today. Compared with our absorption of the world's news through all the media, our continual entertainment by newspapers, radio and/or television, how little time do most of us spend on absorbing the truths of God? It is by this absorption that we grow spiritually and develop our 'salvation'.

Christ is the 'living stone', both foundation stone and corner stone to the Christian. Peter is here inviting the new-born Christians to let themselves be built into the new House of God as 'living stones' – part of the fabric in which 'holy priests' can offer sacrifices that God will accept. All this is foretold by Isaiah (28:16) – probably quoted here from memory. (See also Psalm 118:22.)

The 'Stone' is a treasure of infinite worth to the believer, but remains a stumbling-block (something to trip over) and thus an offence to those who do not believe. It is highly unfashionable, and even considered 'uncharitable' today to say what Peter plainly states here : the real reason for unbelief is often unwillingness to obey God.

The Gentiles who in the Old Testament were 'non-people' (see Romans 9:25) are now inheriting all the old promised titles of God's chosen people. Gratitude for all these invaluable promises can be best expressed by demonstrating in life the consequences of being called from the darkness of ignorance into the 'amazing light' of the gospel.

Your behaviour . . .

vs 11, 12 I beg you, as those whom I love, to live in this world as strangers and 'temporary residents', to keep clear of the desires of your lower natures, for they are always at war with your souls. Your conduct among the surrounding peoples in your different countries should always be good and right, so that although they may slander you as evil-doers yet when troubles come, they may glorify God when they see how well you conduct yourselves.

'Desires of your lower natures'. This ethical teaching is not new; it is at least as old as Plato. Paul expresses the battle between the 'flesh' and the 'spirit' (not 'soul') more definitely and more accurately, theologically speaking, in Romans 7, especially in the closing verses of that chapter. Possibly Peter is here using phraseology which was familiar, however little the ethic was put into practice, in the pagan world.

'Your conduct'. Christians, for various and often slanderous reasons, were beginning to get a dubious or bad name. All the more reason then for living a life irreproachable in the eyes of God. Justice will one day prevail and their lives will then be seen to be truly good. Surely in today's world with its false values and mixed priorities we must be faithful, always, to what we know is good and right.

... to the outside world

vs 13–17 Obey every man-made authority for the Lord's sake – whether it is the emperor, as the supreme ruler, or the governors whom he has appointed to punish evil-doers and reward those who do good service. It is the will of God that you may thus silence the ill-informed criticisms of the foolish. As free men you should never use your freedom as a screen for doing wrong, but live as servants of God. You should have respect for everyone, you should love our brotherhood, fear God and honour the emperor.

The Christian is not normally called to be a 'drop-out' or an anarchist. His best defence against slander and abuse was, and is, the steady witness of a good life. So far as conscience allows he is to obey authority on the grounds that all authority derives from God. It is only when, for example, the Roman emperor considers himself divine and demands not obedience but *worship* that the Christians must refuse. This was the major cause of the most cruel and relentless persecution of the early Church.

We are today required to be law-abiding citizens, giving honour and respect where they are due. It is only when the government or state directly contradicts the laws of God that the Christian must protest or, in the last resort, disobey. Such non-violent disobedience has been and is practised by various brave men and women in many countries of the world today, not only in professedly atheistic communities but also under so-called Christian authority.

A word to household servants

vs 18–25 You who are servants should submit to your masters with proper respect – not only to the good and kind, but also to the difficult. A man does a fine thing

when he endures pain, with a clear conscience towards
God, though he knows he is suffering unjustly. After all,
it is no credit to you if you are patient in bearing a
punishment which you have richly deserved! But if you
do your duty and are punished for it and can still accept
it patiently, you are doing something worthwhile in God's
sight. Indeed this is your calling. For Christ suffered for
you and left you a personal example, so that you might
follow in his footsteps. He was guilty of no sin nor of the
slightest prevarication. Yet when he was insulted he
offered no insult in return. When he suffered he made no
threats of revenge. He simply committed his cause to
the One who judges fairly. And he personally bore our
sins in his own body on the cross, so that we might be
dead to sin and be alive to all that is good. It was the
suffering that he bore which has healed you. You had
wandered away like so many sheep, but now you have
returned to the shepherd and guardian of your souls.

'Servants'. These are household servants, 'domestics', probably
but not necessarily, slaves. They were often 'freed' men and
women who stayed on in their master's household.

'Difficult' – literally 'perverse'. The nearly impossible course
of action recommended here is 'a fine thing' for the best of all
possible reasons; it is a conforming to the pattern of Christ's
own earthly life.

'This is your calling'. Very rarely does the New Testament
tell us to consider Christ as a 'personal example'; but here
certainly. Which of us has not had to deal with the 'difficult'
– in personal relationships, in the business world, or even in
marriage? A simple reading of this masterly summary of
Christ's attitude in an evil world will do something to calm
our exasperated souls. Not only Example but Redeemer and
Saviour. We are never allowed to forget this in the New
Testament.

'On the cross' could be translated 'on to' or 'to the cross', expressing the ultimate limit to which incarnate love could go. The metaphors used here are, of course, strongly reminiscent of the Old Testament (see especially Isaiah 53), with all its teaching on sin-bearing atonement and the virtues of sacrifice. All these ideas are more than fulfilled by Jesus Christ; they are indeed superseded. However variously men may interpret Christ's act of reconciliation in his work of redemption (and there are at least a dozen theories of atonement) sooner or later we have to drop our efforts at self-justification. That which we could never do *has been done.* Millions of Christians have accepted this supreme act of loving redemption and have found 'peace with God'. Quite literally there is no other way; it is a bitter blow to human pride but this is the only inescapable first step.

CHAPTER THREE

*

A word to married Christians

vs 1–7 In the same spirit you married women should adapt yourselves to your husbands, so that even if they do not obey the Word of God they may be won to God without any word being spoken, simply by seeing the pure and reverent conduct of you, their wives. Your beauty should not be dependent on an elaborate coiffure, or on the wearing of jewellery or fine clothes, but on the inner personality – the unfading loveliness of a calm and gentle spirit, a thing very precious in the eyes of God. This was the beauty of the holy women of ancient times who trusted in God and were submissive to their husbands. Sarah, you will remember, obeyed Abraham and called him her lord. And you have become her true descendants today as long as you too live good lives and do not give way to hysterical fears.

Similarly, you husbands should try to understand the
wives you live with, honouring them as physically weaker
yet equally heirs with you of the grace of life. If you
don't do this, you will find it impossible to pray together
properly.

'Adapt yourselves'. The Greek word means literally 'arrange
yourselves under', possibly a military word used for an officer
who 'arranged' his forces 'under' his general. The thought is
not one of slavish submission, hence this attempt to paraphrase
in modern English.

Mixed marriages would be as common in these scattered
communities as in Corinth, where Paul's letters lay down
certain 'guide-lines'. The woman's witness and influence is the
most potent way of 'winning' an unbelieving husband.

'Your beauty', etc. Fairly obvious to the modern Christian,
but a new thought to ex-pagans. The ancient world set great
store by personal adornment. This little passage may seem
irrelevant to us. The point the writer is trying to make is that
just as men are, through Christ, 'sons of Abraham', so women
may, by their attitude and behaviour, be true daughters of
Sarah, Abraham's wife. Paul lifts the matter to a much higher
plane when he declares that 'in Christ there is neither male
nor female . . .' (Galatians 3:28).

The corollary of the wife's adaptation to her husband's
authority is naturally the latter's understanding and honour of
his wife.

'Grace of life'. This could mean sharing the beauties and
joys, as well as the grace God gives, in this life. Or possibly,
it means a sharing in the promises of the life to come.

'Pray together'. The end of verse 7 is literally true.

Be good to each other – and to all men

vs 8–12 To sum up, you should all be of one mind living
like brothers with true love and sympathy for each other,

compassionate and humble. Never pay back a bad turn
with a bad turn or an insult with another insult, but on
the contrary pay back with good. For this is your calling
– to do good and to inherit the goodness of God. For :
  He that would love life,
  And see good days,
  Let him refrain his tongue from evil,
  And his lips that they speak no guile :
  And let him turn away from evil, and do good;
  Let him seek peace and pursue it.
  For the eyes of the Lord are upon the righteous,
  And his ears unto their supplication :
  But the face of the Lord is against them that do evil.

The new spirit that should pervade the Christian community.

'Humble', a Greek adjective not found elsewhere, I think,
in the New Testament, is difficult to translate. Perhaps
'modest in mind' comes a little nearer to the true meaning.

'Never pay back', etc. An echo of Jesus' teaching (Matthew
5:43–8). Verses 10–12 are a quotation from the Septuagint
(i.e. Greek) version of Psalm 34:12–16. The Greek is a little
stronger than the English – literally 'he who wills to love
life.'

Do good, . . .

vs 13–16 After all, who is likely to injure you for being
devoted to what is good? And if it should happen that
you suffer for living a good life you are fortunate. You
need neither fear men's threats nor worry about them;
simply concentrate on being completely devoted to Christ
in your hearts. Be ready at any time to give a quiet and
reverent answer to any man who wants a reason for the
hope that you have within you. Make sure that your
conscience is perfectly clear, so that if men should speak
slanderously of you as rogues they may come to feel

ashamed of themselves for abusing you for your good Christian behaviour.

It was by this time probably an offence to practise the Christian religion but there would have to be an 'informer' before prosecution could start. So far, apparently, this was unlikely to happen. The good law-abiding life, full of joy and hope, was the best attitude for the Christian.

'Quiet and reverent answer'. Some Christians, even today, are arrogant and boastful; they alone know the truth, and they are faintly contemptuous of unbelievers. But this is no true expression of the Christian faith; no man has ever been won to the faith in Christ by another's 'superiority'. The Christian's behaviour in the surrounding community must be blameless. Such living is only made possible by the power of Christ, demonstrated by his defeat of death and by his return to majesty, and now operating in the hearts of those who believe in him.

... even if you suffer for it

vs 17–22 If it is the will of God that you should suffer it is better to suffer for doing good than for doing wrong. Remember that Christ the just suffered for us the unjust, to bring us to God. That meant the death of his body, but he was brought to life again in the spirit. It was in the spirit that he went and preached to the imprisoned souls of those who had been disobedient in the days of Noah – the days of God's great patience during the period of the building of the ark, in which eventually only eight souls were saved from the water. That water was a kind of prophetic parable of the water of baptism which now saves you. Baptism does not merely mean the washing of a dirty body; it is the appeal of a clear conscience towards God – a thing made possible by the power of Christ's resurrection. For he has now entered

Heaven and sits at God's right hand, with all angels, authorities and powers made subject to him.

'Better'. This seems a strange word to use here. But it is perfectly consonant with the teaching of Jesus (Matthew 5:10), and with his own example. Evil can never be conquered by evil, and the cost is high. It can only be done in the power of Christ. 'Overpower evil with good!' (Romans 12:21).

Death appeared to conquer Christ physically, but he defeated death spiritually.

During the two and a half days of earth-time that Jesus' body was in the tomb Peter asserts here that 'in the spirit' Jesus went and proclaimed the message of God's love to those who had lived and died in previous centuries, and who were now 'imprisoned' in Hades or Sheol. They were thus given an opportunity to repent and turn to the living God. Before we dismiss this as mere myth, as some do, it is well to remember that we know nothing about life outside the 'space-time' existence of this planet. Step outside this and neither 'time' nor 'space' have any meaning. Thus Peter may well have been reporting as best he could within his human limits, a real, but very mysterious event.

The thought of Noah brings Peter back to more familiar thought. The waters of the Flood were to him a pre-figuring of the waters of baptism. Washing with water means far more than the cleansing of the body; it is the outward sign of a clean inner attitude towards God. This latter, which is no less a miracle, is made possible by the same power which raised Jesus from the dead and restored him to his position of power and authority in the timeless world of what we call, for want of a better word, 'Heaven'. We seem for the most part to be a little short of experimental knowledge of this power. It shines and blazes in the pages of the New Testament and Christ cannot have changed.

CHAPTER FOUR

*

Following Christ will mean pain

vs 1–6 Since Christ suffered physical pain you must arm yourselves with the same inner conviction that he had. To be free from sin means bodily suffering, and the man who accepts this will spend the rest of his time here on earth, not in being led by human desires, but in doing the will of God. Your past life may have been good enough for pagan purposes, though it meant sensuality, lust, drunkenness, orgies, carousals and worshipping forbidden gods. Indeed your former companions may think it very strange that you no longer join with them in their riotous excesses, and accordingly say all sorts of abusive things about you. They are the ones who will have to answer for their behaviour before the One who is prepared to judge all men, living or dead. That is why the dead also had the gospel preached to them. For although they must be condemned for the life they lived in the body of men, they might find life in the spirit by obeying God's will.

'Christ suffered'. This is a further extension of the thoughts on Christ's death. Christ's way of perfect obedience to the Father's will meant suffering, physical, mental and spiritual, to the point of agony and to a shameful and excruciating death. His followers must expect similar suffering, although naturally in a different way. To renounce sin at baptism is one thing; to achieve freedom from sin in life means a painful struggle with some of the basic needs of the body and some clamant demands of the unconverted heart and soul. To some

164

this is a daily unremitting battle, to others the fundamental changeover of inner attitude seems to come more easily. But for all there is no victory except by suffering. The positive side of such a life-long struggle is to do 'the will of God' whatever the cost. There was literally 'plenty of time' in times past for your pagan indulgences. It is quite different now that your eyes are open.

Your changed life may provoke amazement, and hostility, from the pagans among whom you live. You need not be worried by this. All men will face the judgement of Christ, who has been appointed by God as judge of all men.

It is the careless pagan who should be anxious, not you, for you have made your peace with God.

Verse 6 is probably a reference back to 3:19, 20. But this passage has been variously interpreted. It probably was part of the Christian answer to the pagan question, 'if you Christians go to all this trouble to live as God wants you to live, why do you die just as we do?' The early believers would reply that they did indeed die in the body but they were sure of sharing in spirit in the Resurrection of Christ. They would be alive with the timeless life of God himself. Even those who had already died, the writer seems to be saying here, had the opportunity of finding this 'life' when the Gospel was proclaimed to them by the risen Christ.

Your attitude in these last days

vs 7–11 We are near the end of all things now, and you should therefore be calm, self-controlled men of prayer. Above everything else be sure that you have real deep love for each other, remembering how love can cover a multitude of sins. Be hospitable to each other without secretly wishing you hadn't got to be ! Serve one another with the particular gifts God has given each of you, as faithful dispensers of the wonderfully varied grace of God. If any of you is a preacher then he should preach his message as from God. And in whatever way a man serves the Church he should do it recognizing the fact that God gives him his ability, so that God may be glorified in everything through Jesus Christ. To him belong glory and power for ever, amen!

The writer can naturally see no further than his own 'horizon'. Like other New Testament writers he thought the end of all things was near. It wasn't. Yet the hope that Christ will break through into human history at the end of what we call 'time' remains an integral part of the Christian faith. Despite the follies of those who thought that they knew 'the times and seasons' and were proved wrong, the hope remains.

The Christian attitude in any crisis, even the last, should be 'calm' and 'self-controlled'; an attitude maintained by prayer.

Above all things real 'love' for one another must be maintained. 'Love can cover.' This is a reminiscence of Proverbs 10:12, 'Hatred stirreth up strife, but love covereth all sins.' The thought is that in an atmosphere of deep love hatreds dissolve and pride is shed. Offences which would be magnified in an atmosphere of hatred are minimized, overlooked and forgiven in that of love.

The expression of love must show itself in such ordinary things as ungrudging hospitality, as well as in the exercise of God's gifts through his 'wonderfully varied' grace.

If men recognize constantly that their abilities come from God the 'credit' goes to God and not to the human being. And this is surely not only right and proper, but builds a wholesome attitude of mind.

Your attitude to persecution

vs 12–19 And now, dear friends of mine. I beg you not to be unduly alarmed at the fiery ordeals which come to test your faith, as though this were some abnormal experience. You should be glad, because it means that you are sharing in Christ's sufferings. One day, when he shows himself in full splendour, you will be filled with the most tremendous joy. If you are reproached for being Christ's followers, that is a cause for joy, for you can be sure that God's Spirit of glory is resting upon you. But take care that none of your number suffers as a murderer, or a thief, a rogue or a busy-body! If he suffers as a Christian he has nothing to be ashamed of and may glorify God by confessing Christ's name.

The time has evidently arrived for God's judgment to begin, and it is beginning at his own household. And if it starts with us, what is it going to mean to those who refuse to obey the gospel of God? If even the good man is only just saved, what will be the fate of the wicked and the sinner? Therefore those who suffer according to God's will can safely commit their souls to their faithful Creator, and go on doing all the good they can.

These verses could have been added as an urgent postscript. Perhaps Peter, in Rome, knew that the campaign of persecution was about to be 'stepped up', and that the 'fiery ordeals' (not necessarily to be understood literally) might reach the scattered young churches in the near future. Like the tests of faith mentioned in 1:6, 7, the trials of persecution will test and purify faith and faithfulness.

'Christ's sufferings'. Meaning here not the sufferings of Jesus on earth but what the risen Christ suffers as head of his Church. He and the Christian are in closest sympathy. When we suffer for Christ, he suffers with us, and we with him. This thought is worth our serious reflection.

'Tremendous joy'. The time will come when we shall see the purpose and value of all our pain and persecution for Christ's sake. It will be easily seen *then*, but even now it is a 'cause for joy'. When you suffer bravely and cheerfully 'God's Spirit of glory is resting upon you.' It may not feel like that, or look like that, but this is the truth about the matter.

In troubled times, when standards are confused and law and order seem to be breaking down, it is a temptation to lose even ordinary standards of decent human conduct. This has happened in our own day under the horrors of war and the extreme rigours of a prison camp. The only 'offence' the Christian must allow himself to commit is boldly to confess Christ when challenged.

Peter sees the coming conflict of faith with unbelief, of the powers of the Roman Empire with the steadfast loyalty of the young unarmed churches, as 'God's judgment'. This he would naturally do, as one who was brought up on the Old Testament, where the thought is widespread. Such judgment will begin with the testing of 'his own household', that is the Church. It will be hard enough for those who believe, who must continue in steadfast faith and in 'doing all the good they can'. 'What will be the fate of the wicked and the sinner?' A rhetorical question; neither Peter nor we can answer it.

CHAPTER FIVE

*

A word to your leaders

vs 1–4 Now may I who am myself an elder say a word to you my fellow-elders? I speak as one who actually saw Christ suffer, and as one who will share with you the glories that are to be unfolded. Shepherd your flock of God, looking after them not because you feel compelled to, but willingly, as God would wish. Never do this work thinking of your personal gain but with true compassion. You should aim not at being dictators but examples of Christian living in the eyes of the flock committed to your charge. And then, when the Chief Shepherd reveals him-

self, you will receive that crown of glory which cannot
fade.

'An elder'. Peter writes with some modesty! By this time he
had earned great honour and respect. Although most of us
cannot accept the Roman Catholic claims about him, he
unquestionably occupied a position of great spiritual authority
in Rome.

'Fellow-elders'. These were the *presbuteroi* of the local
churches. The Greek word means no more than 'elders', but
it is obvious from this chapter alone that it has already become
a position of authority, carrying with it some financial reward.
'Presbyter', and later in the Anglican Church 'Priest', are both
derived from the Greek *presbuteros*.

Such men are urged to 'shepherd' their flock willingly and
with compassion. They are not to seek power or gain but
aim to be 'examples of Christian living'.

The idea of a 'shepherd and his flock' occurs much in the
Old Testament (remember Psalm 23), and was taken over by
Christ in the words recorded in John 10. Now, risen in
majesty, he is 'the Chief Shepherd' who will reward the
faithful.

Learn to be humble and to trust

vs 5–7 You younger members must also accept the
authority of the elders. Indeed all of you should defer
to one another and wear the 'overall' of humility in
serving each other. God is always against the proud, but
he is always ready to give grace to the humble. So,
humble yourselves under God's strong hand, and in his
own good time he will lift you up. You can throw the
whole weight of your anxieties upon him, for you are his
personal concern.

'Overall'. An attempt by the translator, by a pardonable pun, to convey the completeness of the clothing of humility. Proud men do not wear overalls.

'Against the proud' literally, 'God is organized against the proud' – that is his permanent attitude.

'Throw the whole weight'. The verb used here is a violent one, as describing a man getting rid of an intolerable burden.

'His personal concern'. We have today a far bigger and wider concept of God and his creation than Peter could ever have had. The penalty for this is that it becomes very much harder for an individual to believe in God's personal concern for him. Harder for him, but of course it presents no difficulty to the infinite wisdom and love of God! Probably the most vivid paraphrase is still 'it matters to him about you', but I have been unable to trace its source.

Resist the devil: you are in God's hands

vs 8–11 Be self-controlled and vigilant always, for your enemy the devil is always about, prowling like a lion roaring for its prey. Resist him, standing firm in your faith, remembering that the strain is the same for all your fellow-Christians in other parts of the world. And after you have borne these sufferings a very little while, the God of all grace, who has called you to share his eternal splendour through Christ, will himself make you whole and secure and strong. All power is his for ever and ever, amen!

'Roaring for its prey', better 'looking for someone to devour'. It is the weakest of the flock or herd who fall victim to the prowling predator. By prayer and vigilance, by steadfast, faithful resistance to the powers of evil you will be safe. All Christians anywhere in the world share the strain of this battle in one form or another. We cannot avoid it in the world of today.

'Make you whole', literally 'adjust you'. The living Spirit

of God is always 'adjusting' Christians who are sensitive to his lead. Probably Peter is referring here to the final 'adjustment' in Heaven, where we shall all be made 'whole'.

Final greetings

vs 12–14   I am sending this short letter by Silvanus, whom I know to be a faithful brother, to stimulate your faith and assure you that the above words represent the true grace of God. See that you stand fast in that grace!

Your sister-church here in 'Babylon' sends you greetings, and so does my son Mark. Give each other a handshake all round as a sign of love.

Peace be to all true Christians.

'Silvanus'. This is the Latin form of the Greek 'Silas'. If he is the Silas mentioned in the Acts he was Paul's companion and was named by him in both his letters to the Thessalonians. Silas was probably Peter's secretary and actually wrote this letter, as he may well have written for Paul.

'Babylon'. The actual city had long since sunk into oblivion. But it was a common 'archetype', especially to Jews, of a pagan city. All Peter's readers would know that he was speaking of Rome and of the church there.

'My son Mark'. Probably meaning no more than an expression of affection, such as Paul had for both Timothy and Titus. There is no reason to doubt that this man is John Mark of the Gospels and Acts.

'A handshake'. This is of course literally 'a kiss' but the translator felt this would jar on modern ears. The 'kiss of Christian love' occurs several times in the New Testament letters but it was later discarded as churches grew from small communities to larger and more complex organizations.

'Peace'. The old Jewish greeting took on a fresh meaning to the Christians who knew 'peace with God' and 'the peace which passes all understanding'.

THE
SECOND LETTER OF
PETER

CHAPTER ONE

*

vs 1, 2 Simon Peter, a servant and messenger of Jesus
Christ, sends this letter to those who have been given a
faith as valuable as ours in the righteousness of our God,
and saviour Jesus Christ. May you know more and more
of grace and peace as your knowledge of God and Jesus
our Lord grows deeper.

'Servant and messenger'. Literally this means 'slave and
apostle'. This combination of utter humility and divinely
appointed commission is used also by Paul.

'Righteousness'. Either the character of the just God is
meant here or the 'righteousness' produced by him in the life
of the believer.

'God and saviour' could both grammatically refer to Jesus
Christ, but probably the reference is to God the Father and
to Jesus Christ the Son.

'More and more'. This is an echo of 1 Peter 1:2, with the
addition of a prayer for deeper 'knowledge' *Epignosis* in the
Greek means 'recognition'.

God has done his part: see that you do yours

vs 3–11 He has by his own action given us everything
that is necessary for living the truly good life, in allowing
us to know the one who has called us to him, through his
own glorious goodness. It is through this generosity that
God's greatest and most precious promises have become
available to us men, making it possible for you to escape
the inevitable disintegration that lust produces in the

175

world and to share in God's essential nature. For this very reason you must do your utmost from your side, and see that your faith carries with it real goodness of life. Your goodness must be accompanied by knowledge, your knowledge by self-control, your self-control by the ability to endure. Your endurance too must always be accompanied by devotion to God; that in turn must have in it the quality of brotherliness, and your brotherliness must lead on to Christian love. If you have these qualities existing and growing in you then it means that knowing our Lord Jesus Christ has not made your lives either complacent or unproductive. The man whose life fails to exhibit these qualities is blind – his eyes so closed that he has forgotten that he was cleansed from his former sins.

Set your minds, then, on endorsing by your conduct the fact that God has called and chosen you. If you go along these lines there is no reason why you should stumble. Indeed if you live this sort of life a rich welcome awaits you as you enter the eternal kingdom of our Lord and saviour Jesus Christ.

It is God's 'generosity' which makes salvation possible.

'Lust' is here used in the broadest sense, meaning the 'selfish greed' that leads to the breakdown of human society.

'You must do your utmost'. It is not enough for God to be loving and generous; man must respond with all his strength.

This formidable list of virtues (vs 6, 7) is worth reading slowly. They can be seen in the lives of committed Christians today.

'Existing and growing'. The true Christian has these virtues permanently, and they grow as he grows.

'Blind'. Probably it would be better to add 'or short-sighted'. Such a man has 'taken forgetfulness' (an odd expression in Greek) of his past.

'Set your minds'. The Christian's concentration is on Christian living, and at the end of the road he is sure of 'a rich welcome' into the eternal Kingdom.

Truth will bear repetition

vs 12–19 Therefore I shall not fail to remind you again and again of things like this although you know them and are already established in the truth which has come to you. I consider it my duty, as long as I live in the temporary dwelling of this body, to stimulate you by these reminders. I know that I shall have to leave this body at very short notice, as our Lord Jesus Christ made clear to me. Consequently I shall make the most of every opportunity, so that after I am gone you will remember these things.

We were not following a cleverly written-up story when we told you about the power and presence of our Lord Jesus Christ – we actually saw his majesty with our own eyes. He received honour and glory from God the Father himself when that voice said to him, out of the sublime glory of Heaven, 'This is my beloved Son, in whom I am well pleased.' We actually heard that voice speaking from Heaven while we were with him on the sacred mountain. Thus we hold the word of prophecy to be more certain than ever. You should give that word your closest attention, for it shines like a lamp amidst the darkness of the world, until the day dawns, and the morning star rises in your hearts.

'Temporary dwelling'. Literally this means a 'tabernacle' or 'booth'. The imagery follows Paul in 2 Corinthians 5:1. It is possible that, since a brief account of the Transfiguration shortly follows, there is a connection between the 'tabernacles' Peter wanted to put up then. He now knows that the true 'tabernacle' is his own physical body.

'As our Lord Jesus Christ'. This implies some private message regarding Peter's death. Paul seems to have had a similar intimation, see Philippians 1:23–25.

'We actually saw'. There is no need for a 'cleverly written-up story' when an eye-witness is available. And, moreover, the experience was endorsed by a voice from Heaven.

'The word of prophecy'. This means God's Word, whether heard from Heaven or spoken by the prophets in the name of the Lord.

False prophets will flourish, but only for a time

vs 20, 21 But you must understand that this is of the highest importance : no prophecy of scripture can be interpreted by a single human mind. No prophecy came because a man wanted it to : men of God spoke because they were inspired by the Holy Spirit.

'A single human mind'. Or 'no prophecy has its own individual solution'. Every genuine word from God must be seen and interpreted in the context of what God has said and is saying.

CHAPTER TWO

*

vs 1–9 But even in those days there were false prophets among the people, just as there will be false teachers among you today. They will be men who will subtly introduce dangerous heresies. They will thereby deny the Lord who redeemed them, and it will not be long before they bring on themselves their own downfall. Many will follow their flagrant immorality and thereby bring dis-

credit on the way of truth. In their lust to make converts
these men will try to exploit you too with their bogus
arguments. But judgment has been for some time hard
on their heels and their downfall is inevitable. For if God
did not spare angels who sinned against him, but
banished them to the dark imprisonment of hell till
judgment day; if he did not spare the ancient world but
only saved Noah, the solitary voice that cried out for
righteousness, and his seven companions when he
brought the flood upon the world in its wickedness; and
if God reduced the entire cities of Sodom and Gomorrah
to ashes, when he sentenced them to destruction as a
fearful example to those who wanted to live in defiance
of his laws, and yet saved Lot the righteous man, in
acute mental distress at the filthy lives of the godless –
Lot, remember, was a good man suffering spiritual
agonies day after day at what he saw and heard of their
lawlessness – then you may be absolutely certain that the
Lord knows how to rescue good men surrounded by
temptation, and how to reserve his punishment for the
wicked until their day comes.

The author of this chapter is carried away by his passion
against false teachers. To him they are all immoral, arrogant,
false and mercenary.

'Did not spare angels', etc. It looks very much as if the
writer of this letter had that of Jude before him. See Jude
6–11. The writer quotes the judgments of God shown in the
days of Noah and in the days of Lot when Sodom and
Gomorrah were utterly destroyed. If this letter were designed,
as was 1 Peter, for converted pagans, it seems a little doubtful
whether they would be impressed by examples from ancient
Jewish history.

'How to rescue'. This is relevant and understandable.
Christians were by now (in the second century) facing all sorts
of pressures, persecutions and gross misunderstandings from

the surrounding world. They needed to be reminded of the Lord who 'knows how to rescue good men surrounded by temptation'.

Let me show you what these men are really like

vs 10–22 His judgment is chiefly reserved for those who have indulged all the foulness of their lower natures, and have nothing but contempt for authority. These men are arrogant and presumptuous – they think nothing of scoffing at the glories of the unseen world. Yet even angels, who are their superiors in strength and power, do not bring insulting criticisms of such things before the Lord.

But these men, with no more sense than the unreasoning brute beasts which are born to be caught and killed, scoff at things outside their own experience, and will most certainly be destroyed in their own corruption. Their wickedness has earned them an evil end and they will be paid in full.

These are the men who delight in daylight self-indulgence; they are foul spots and blots, playing their tricks at your very dinner-tables. Their eyes cannot look at a woman without lust, and they miss no opportunity for sin. They captivate the unstable ones, and their technique of getting what they want is, through long practice, highly developed. They are born under a curse, for they have abandoned the right road and wandered off to follow the old trail of Balaam, son of Beor, the man who had no objection to wickedness as long as he was paid for it. But he, you remember, was sharply reprimanded for his wickedness – by a donkey, of all things, speaking with a human voice to check the prophet's wicked infatuation!

These men are like wells without a drop of water in them, like the changing shapes of whirling storm-clouds, and their fate will be the black night of utter darkness.

With their high-sounding nonsense they use the sensual pull of the lower passions to attract those who were just on the point of cutting loose from their companions in evil. They promise them liberty. Liberty! – when they themselves are bound hand and foot to utter depravity. For a man is the slave of whatever masters him. If men have escaped from the world's contaminations through knowing our Lord and saviour Jesus Christ, and then become entangled and defeated by them all over again, their last position is worse than their first. For it would be better for them not to have known the way of goodness at all, than after knowing it to turn their backs on the sacred commandments given to them. For them, the old proverbs have come true about the 'dog returning to his vomit', and 'the sow that had been washed going back to wallow in the muck'.

This is really a more highly coloured version of the condemnation of false teachers in the letter of Jude. The language is high-pitched, rhetorical and bombastic. It would be far more effective if it did not indulge in wild generalizations and 'came down to cases'.

'Balaam'. See Numbers 22.

'Wells without a drop of water'. A more lurid version of Jude 12 and 13.

'Their last position is worse'. This at least is true, and has been true throughout the Church's history. The 'lapsed Christian' is far more difficult to reach with the Gospel than the hungry, and possibly wistful, pagan.

A pessimistic note, sounding as if it were inevitable that men should return to their unconverted human nature. But it is surely only inevitable if the grace of God is flouted and denied.

CHAPTER THREE

*

God delays the last day, in his mercy

vs 1–10 This is the second letter I have written to you, dear friends of mine, and in both of them I have tried to stimulate you, as men with minds uncontaminated by error, by reminding you of what you really know already. This means recalling the words spoken of old by the holy prophets as well as the commands of our Lord and saviour given to you through his messengers.

First of all you must realize that in the last days cynical mockers will undoubtedly come – men whose only guide in life is what they want for themselves – and they will say, 'Where is his promised coming? Since our fathers fell asleep, everything remains exactly as it was since the beginning of creation!' They are deliberately shutting their eyes to the fact that there were heavens in the old days and an earth formed by God's command out of water and by water. It was by water that the world of those days was deluged and destroyed, but the present heavens and earth are, also by God's command, being carefully kept and maintained for the fire of the day of judgment and the destruction of wicked men.

But you should never lose sight of this fact, dear friends, that with the Lord a day may be a thousand years, and a thousand years only a day. It is not that he is dilatory about keeping his own promise as some men seem to think; the fact is that he is very patient with you. He has no wish that any man should be destroyed; he wishes that all men should find the way to repentance. Yet the day of the Lord will come as unexpectedly as a thief. In that day the heavens will vanish in a tearing blast, the very elements will disintegrate in heat and the earth and all its works will disappear.

'This is the second letter'. We do not know whether the writer of this letter had written a previous one, now lost. He may have been referring to the first letter of Peter, though he does not otherwise mention it. It *may* have been a rather unpleasant attempt to secure the accepted authority of 1 Peter for this letter, which was long regarded as dubious by the early Church.

'Recalling'. Christians may look to the true prophets of old as well as to remembered, or written, words of 'our Lord and saviour'. They do today. This is the real point of 'Bible reading' : to stimulate the mind in faith.

'His messengers' would be more accurately 'your apostles', which makes it appear as if the present writer is not an 'apostle' and is referring to earlier teaching.

'Where is his promised coming?' The burden of much of the New Testament letters' emphasis on a good and healthy spiritual life is because the return of Christ is imminent. Paul certainly stresses this in his earlier letters. But now the 'cynical mockers' consider this promise as discredited – for by now a generation had lived and died – and with it the faith and moral order practised by Christians. If that promise remains unfulfilled why believe any of the others?

It is strange that the writer of this letter does not quote the promises of Jesus himself, for he certainly spoke of his personal return. Instead he concentrates on the fact that 'time' is not reckoned in human terms by God. His apparent dilatoriness can be understood in terms of his patience and unwillingness to condemn.

The water of the deluge was to him one instance of God's judgment; the present age is destined to be destroyed by fire. 'Elements will disintegrate'. This may be thought of as an uncanny and uncomfortable prophetic guess for us who live in a 'nuclear age'! But such expressions were quite common in 'apocalyptic' literature. Fearful floods, devastating pestilence and a final all-consuming fire were a not unusual picture.

Never lose sight of the eternal world

vs 11–13 In view of the fact that all these things are to be dissolved, what sort of people ought you to be? Surely men of good and holy character, who live expecting and working for the coming of the day of God. This day will mean that the heavens will disintegrate in fire and burning elements will melt, but our hopes are set on new heavens and a new earth which he has promised us, in which justice will make its home.

Now the emphasis is changed. A good and holy life is called for, not only because of Christ's undoubted return (though that will 'come as unexpectedly as a thief') but because the whole of the present earthly set-up is temporary and consumable. So it is, sooner or later. No Christian would be so foolish as to rest his final hopes on human life on this planet. He works and prays that God's kingdom may come in the lives of men, but he also awaits in confidence the 'new heavens and a new earth'.

Final words of advice

vs 14–16 Because, my dear friends, you have a hope like this before you, I urge you to make certain that the day will find you at peace with God, flawless and blameless in his sight. Meanwhile, consider that our Lord's patience is for man's salvation, as our dear brother Paul pointed out in his letter to you, written out of the wisdom God gave him. This is how he writes in all his letters when he refers to these things. There are some points in his letters which are difficult to understand, and which ill-informed and unbalanced people distort (as they do the other scriptures), and bring disaster on their own heads.

God's patience is for our salvation, as Paul pointed out in Romans 2:4. See also Ephesians 1:14, 2:7, 3:9–11, which might be considered as written especially for the churches in Asia.

'Difficult to understand'. In ancient times obscurity was sometimes regarded as a virtue, as only hard work would reveal the secret of the teaching. But there was always the danger of shallow and misinformed interpretation by the ignorant and prejudiced. Such faulty understanding could lead to disaster.

'How he writes'. The use of the present tense is not to be taken as meaning that Paul's letters were already being accepted as Scripture.

Keep your proper foothold

vs 17, 18 But you, my friends whom I love, are fore-warned, and should therefore be very careful not to be carried away by the errors of unprincipled men and so lose your proper foothold. On the contrary, you should grow in grace and in knowledge of our Lord and saviour Jesus Christ – to him the glory now and until the day of eternity!

'Errors of unprincipled men'. The 'proper foothold' of the second-century Christians was the teaching of Christ and of the apostles, by now embodied in the teaching of the Church. They must be faithful to this foundation and not be 'carried away' by the errors of men. My personal view is that we should do well to heed this warning today.

'Grow in grace and in knowledge'. A happy description of the progress of a Christian as he matures.